AF441751

Death & Diamonds

The Story of Samuel Soldinger
A Legacy of Oskar Schindler

A Holocaust Survivor's Inspiring Journey of Survival
Faith, Hope, Luck and the American Dream

By Laura Soldinger Yotter and Valerie Lee

Table of Contents

DEDICATION

This book is dedicated to my honorable and loving father, Samuel Soldinger, who shared his inconceivable experiences during the Holocaust. He never gave up hope, attributed his survival to luck, and went on to lead an incredible, joyous, giving, wonderful life. He was an inspiration to the many lives he touched. This is also dedicated to the more than 6 million Jews and others who endured or perished from the atrocities of the Holocaust. This is to honor you, teach others and spread love, kindness, healing and hope for brighter tomorrows for generations to come. May we never forget.

Laura Soldinger Yotter

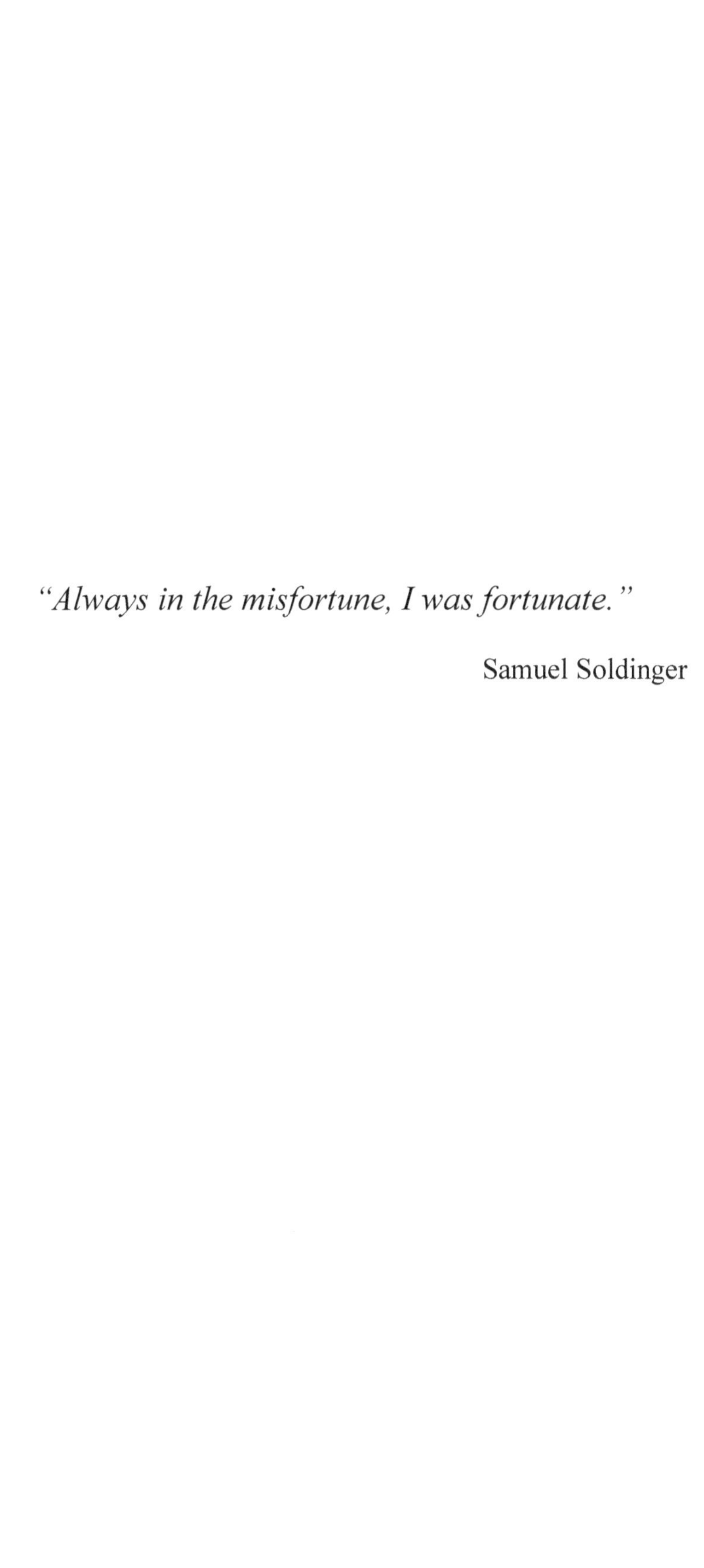

"Always in the misfortune, I was fortunate."

Samuel Soldinger

INTRODUCTION

The facets of a diamond reflect light in 1,000 different ways.

Diamonds - rare, pure and brilliant – are considered to be the hardest known substance. After suffering the horrors of the Holocaust, perhaps it is a beautiful paradox that Samuel Soldinger spent an illustrious career in the diamond industry. Maybe without knowing it, with his kind humility and all he endured, he embodied those same qualities: rarity, purity, brilliance and strength.

It is fascinating, the capacity of the human spirit to remain positive, despite adversity. It could be considered amazing to remain hopeful and pure of heart, despite atrocities the eyes cannot unsee or forget. While the bruises healed, Sam's scars remained, yet he did not let them destroy him and consciously chose to rise above it all.

This book is a compilation of stories mostly in Sam Soldinger's own words, from numerous print and audio interviews, speeches to organizations, along with the notes he kept. There was no one better to tell Sam's experience, than Sam himself, and we are fortunate to have his authentic narrative. This chronicles his time as a young boy growing up in the Jewish Quarter of Krakow, to being a prisoner in seven concentration camps during the German occupation in Poland and Austria during World War II, then onto a life as a diamond cutter for Harry Winston working with Native Americans in Arizona. He was a devoted family man, a doting father, a ping-pong champion and lover of the lights of Las Vegas. Throughout, Sam lived his life with positivity and purpose.

Powerful and poignant, ultimately Sam's is a story of perseverance. It is a testament to how much punishment a person can withstand and to flourish beyond those harrowing days to brighter new ones. This is his story of survival and the American dream. It was with his courage and dignity that the six years of unthinkable brutality did not break the spirit of this sweet, strong and gentle giant.

Sam Soldinger was born in Krakow, Poland on August 28, 1924. Sam's family was Jewish. He was the middle child with one older brother and one younger sister. Little did Sam know that by the age of 17, he would be the only survivor of his immediate family. His father died of complications of diabetes when Sam was 9 years old. His brother escaped to Russia during the war and was never heard from again. Sam's mother and sister were murdered by the Nazis. Sam Soldinger was a "Schindler Jew," saved by Oskar Schindler working in his enamel factory and considered Schindler to be the greatest man who ever lived.

Through Sam's stories, many of which are excruciatingly painful and yet need to be heard, it is clear that he attributed his survival to luck. One would bet how he came away from it was much more than that. How he survived it all, and remained kindhearted and seemingly unscarred, is something to behold. Sam wanted to share his experiences so that they may be a reminder that this never happen to anyone else, any group of people or any other generation. Goodness, compassion and faith shall always prevail, despite everything else in what was a time of unimaginable evil.

To Sam, who has since left us and died peacefully at the age of 76 on January 2, 2001, we thank you for sharing your perilous journey to the lowest depths of humanity, and onto the highest, glorious mountaintop of your freedom, safety and happiness for many years after the war. You were a true inspiration. You, and those alongside you, will never be forgotten. Just as a diamond represents love forever, may love and peace also be forever with you, Samuel Soldinger. Shalom.

EARLY FAMILY LIFE, JEWISH LIFE IN KRAKOW

I was born in Krakow, Malopolskie, Poland on August 28, 1924. All my ancestors that I know were born there. My grandfather and great grandfather were born in Krakow. I am the son of Solomon Jozef Soldinger and Adele Presser Soldinger, and my older brother was Jakob and my younger sister was Sabina.

Soldinger family portrait. Date unknown.

Krakow a beautiful city, a historical city with a tremendous history of Polish kings. In the 1920s and '30s, it was a large, important city that was a center of learning, architecture, arts, culture and sports, and had electric streetlights, streetcars and automobiles. The center of Jewish life in Krakow was the Kazimierz District. The Jewish community there dated back centuries, so it was well established. The entire population of Krakow at the time the war broke out was approximately 250,000 and 60,000 of which were Jews, roughly a quarter of the city's population.

These modern-day maps of Poland illustrate where Poland is in Europe, and where Krakow is within Poland, in the southern part of the country not far from the modern border of Slovakia. Poland is between Germany on the west and the former Soviet states of Belarus and Ukraine on the east.

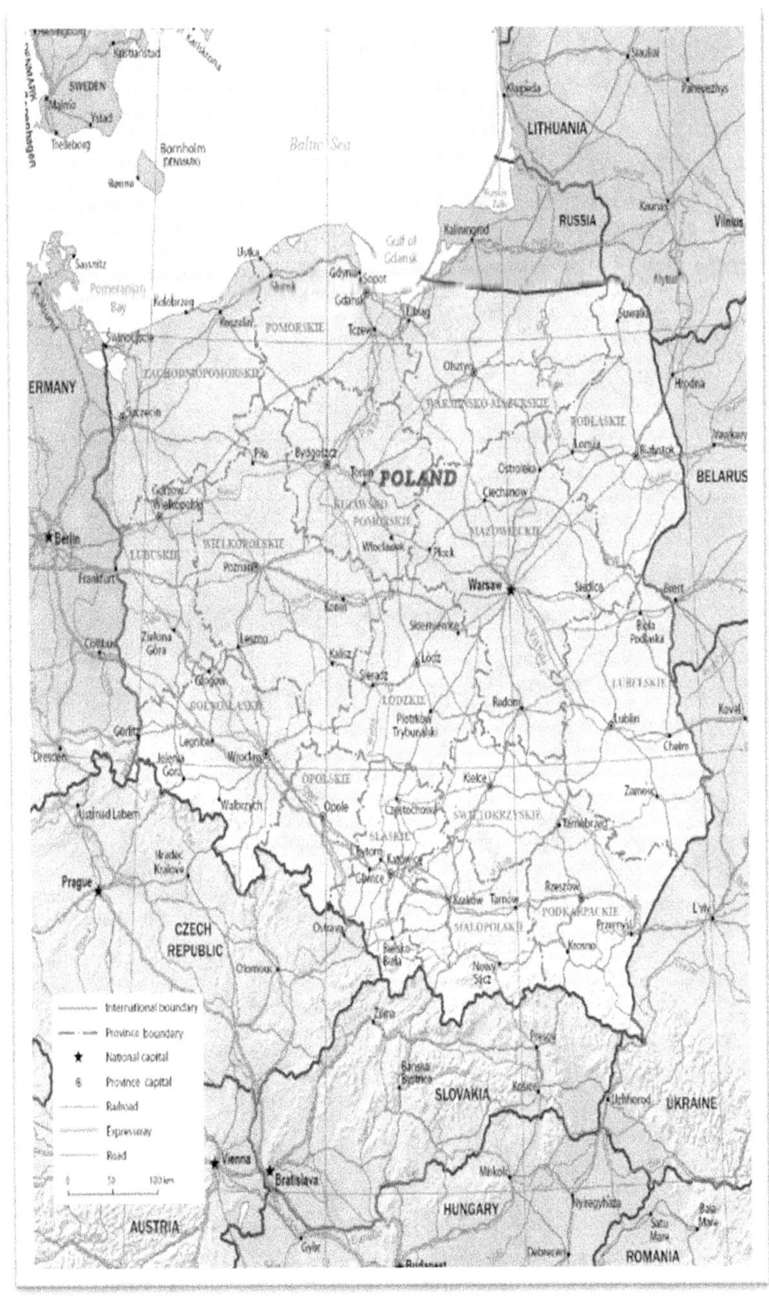

SWEDEN
Kristianstad
Karlskrona
Malmö
Ystad
Trelleborg
Bornholm
(DENMARK)
Rønne
DENMARK
Copenhagen
Baltic Sea
Pomeranian Bay
Sassnitz
Kołobrzeg
Ustka
Gdynia
Sopot
Gulf of Gdansk
Gdansk
Słupsk
Koszalin
Świnoujście
POMORSKIE
Tczew
Elbląg
LITHUANIA
Klaipeda
Palnepezhys
Siauliai
Kaunas
Vilnius
RUSSIA
Kaliningrad
Alytau
Suwałki
GERMANY
Szczecin
ZACHODNIOPOMORSKIE
Olsztyn
WARMIŃSKO-MAZURSKIE
Hrodna
PODLASKIE
Vawkavy
Piła
Bydgoszcz
Łomża
Białystok
Gorzów Wielkopolski
Toruń
POLAND
Ostrołęka
BELARUS
KUJAWSKO-POMORSKIE
Ciechanów
Berlin
WIELKOPOLSKIE
MAZOWIECKIE
Włocławek
Płock
Frankfurt
LUBUSKIE
Poznań
Warsaw
Siedlce
BREST
Konin
Cottbus
Zielona Góra
Leszno
Kalisz
Sieradz
Łódź
Radom
Lublin
Koval
Głogów
ŁÓDZKIE
LUBELSKIE
DOLNOŚLĄSKIE
Piotrków Trybunalski
Görlitz
Legnica
Chełm
Dresden
Jelenia Góra
Wrocław
Kielce
OPOLSKIE
Zamość
Ústí nad Labem
Wałbrzych
Opole
Częstochowa
ŚWIĘTOKRZYSKIE
Tarnobrzeg
ŚLĄSKIE
Hradec Králové
Bytom
Katowice
Gliwice
Prague
Rzeszów
Kraków
Tarnów
Lviv
PODKARPACKIE
Przemyśl
CZECH REPUBLIC
Ostrava
MAŁOPOLSKIE
Krosno
Olomouc
Bielsko-Biała
Nowy Sącz
Žilina
Prešov
Uzhhorod
UKRAINE
Banská Bystrica
Košice
International boundary
Province boundary
National capital
Province capital
Railroad
Expressway
Road
0   50   100 km
SLOVAKIA
Vienna
Bratislava
Miskolc
Nyíregyháza
Baia Mare
AUSTRIA
Győr
HUNGARY
Satu Mare
Debrecen
ROMANIA
Budapest

Krakow is split north and south by the Vistula River, the longest river in Poland. Two important sections of the city were the Kazimierz District, just south of the center of the city. This was the traditional Jewish neighborhood where Sam grew up. Across the river is Podgorze, where the Krakow Ghetto would eventually be established. Between the two districts was Oskar Schindler's enamelware factory, which would play a central role in Sam's ability to survive.

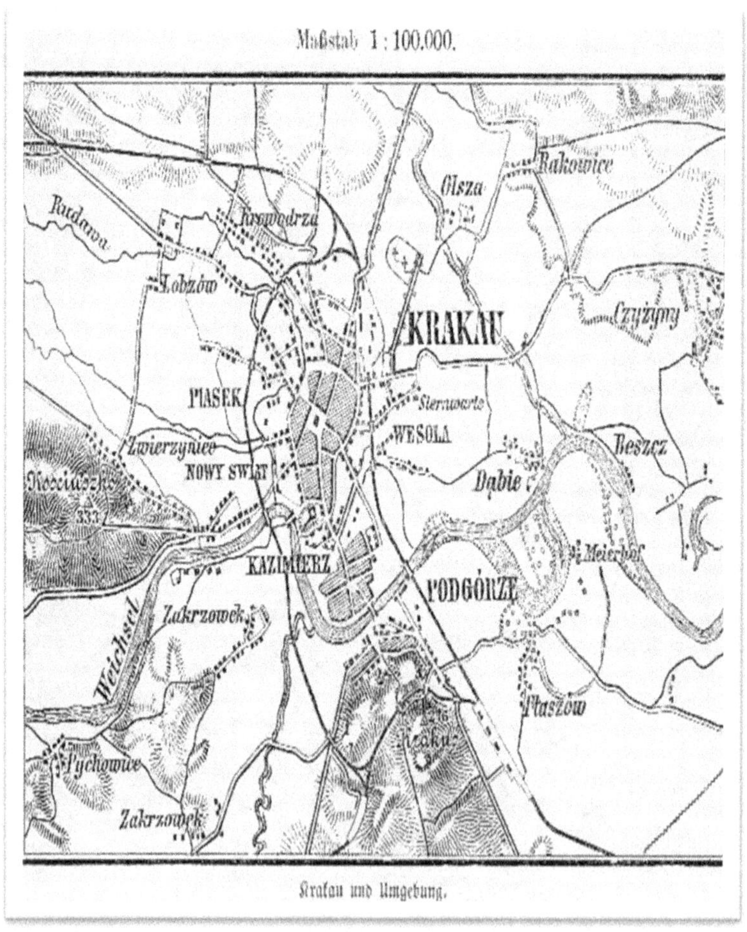

I had a wonderful life here. I had my family, my friends and I went to school. It was a good Jewish life with synagogues and a good environment. The typical neighborhood had stores on the ground floor with apartments above, connected by common balconies.

My father Solomon had a dairy, cheese and butter factory and restaurant he inherited from his father. We were strictly kosher, per Jewish law. Our customers were our neighbors, and at any given time, there might be 20 to 30 people in our restaurant. We had about 20 tables and our refrigeration consisted of iceboxes. My first job when I was 5 or 6 years old, I would seal and stamp bottles of milk and wash the empty bottles people would return.

There were other stores on our block, including Dym's General Store, which was right next to our restaurant that sold candy, fruit and groceries. The Dym's family were Hasidic Jews and very friendly people. There, we bought all of our salt, sugar and staples for our restaurant. Next to Dym's was a stationery store owned by Mr. Newman. Szynk was a nearby restaurant-tavern serving all kosher foods, beer and sweet wines. Their specialty was a honey wine. A barbershop was in the next building. Mr. Schoenwald was the barber and after my father died, he never charged us for haircuts.

My father was always jovial, happy and had many friends. He was very much involved in sports and he would take us to games. He was religious, so we would not go on the Sabbath. He was an amateur poet and some of his poetry was published in the newspaper. He also painted which was marvelous. He always provided charity for the poor by giving them milk, butter and farmer's cheese.

Adele Presser Soldinger and Solomon Jozef Soldinger

My mother, Adele Presser, was born near Krakow and grew up in Wadowice, Poland, where Pope John Paul II was born. (Later in life, we use to say he was our neighbor. I spent a lot of time there and I believe we played ball with him, but cannot say for sure. He was a goalie and we use to pick up people from the street and play soccer. I believe I knew him vaguely.)

We mainly spoke Polish in our home. My family was not particularly religious, but we were Orthodox and Jewish life permeated the neighborhood. My father always wore a hat, and as a child, I always wore a cap. Never without. For the holidays and Shabbat, it was my job to get the meat. We always had a goose or a couple of chickens in the basement. After school on Fridays, I would go to the kosher butcher and my father would go to synagogue. Then on Saturday morning, he went to another synagogue. The milk came from the dairy, and he and the farmers would pray over the milk.

Holidays were formal occasions and we wore proper attire. It was wonderful. Electricity was expensive and my mother would dig out a 100-watt bulb. We had a large trunk of serving plates and dishes and it was a big deal to bring them all out. Of course, I had a favorite coffee mug. The last meal of Passover was a big, poppy seed bagel.

Fun fact: The word bagel comes from Krakow and beygal in Yiddish means ring or bracelet.

The rabbi lived across the street and it was terrific that we had that kind of atmosphere. I used to deliver milk to him daily and he would always tell me what wonderful parents I had.

I had a normal bar mitzvah. All the relatives came and we said a prayer and had a meal. I think it is an exaggerated thing now, bar mitzvahs.

For school, I started at a Hebrew kindergarten and then went to public school, which was prominently Jewish students and mixed teachers. Every day after public school, I went to a Hebrew school in our neighborhood to learn to read Hebrew. Later, I went for two years to technical school, then the war was breaking out and school was cut-off. I was supposed to go a third year. I was studying machinery and tool making. I learned a lot and it helped me a lot later - actually - it saved my life. I am very technically inclined and it helped to later lie to the Germans that I was a terrific machinist, which I was not.

I remember funny childhood moments, like the time I was teased with a ping-pong ball and was told it was a magic egg. So, I figured the opposite must be true! I went and took an egg from the kitchen and threw it down … and it broke. (As an adult, I later became a competitive ping-pong player, so I now know the difference!) Another time, a waitress accidently stepped on and broke my toy flute. Later, when she dropped a dime, I ran away with it and bought a replacement for my flute. Or, there was the time we were in awe when my uncle brought a pineapple to hang in the store. Those were scarce and very expensive. There were moments and memories from my childhood that were normal and happy and just like anyone else. However, there was some anti-Semitism before the war. In my experience as a child, we would be playing ball and sometimes we would get beat up, or have rocks thrown at us and have our ball taken away. Just days before the war, I was in the park on a rainy day with two or three friends. Radical Poles attacked us, and we were beaten black and blue. That was the worst experience I had as a Jew before the war.

Bernard Offen, another survivor of the Krakow Ghetto, was about the same age as Sam. He shared his experiences in a memoir entitled, "My Hometown Concentration Camp." He wrote about the anti-Semitism he endured growing up in Kazimierz. He too recalled that Christian children would chase and throw rocks at him to the point that he feared to even look at the Catholic church as he walked by. This experience was similar to Sam's, which was ominous in retrospect, and helps to explain why many people failed to stand up to the horrors that the Germans inflicted on the Jews and others.

Life really began turning sideways when my father developed diabetes. We had to struggle with the dairy business and my mother worked hard by going to the market at 4 a.m. with cans of milk to sell by the pint or quart. As life got harder, we moved to a room behind our store with a cold-water sink. My mother's legs then became arthritic and we cared for her by keeping her legs warm under a lamp. She was ill and, in the hospital, and my grandmother would come take care of us. Sadly, we ended up losing my father in 1933 when he was 46 years old, my mother was 37 years old and I was nine. He had a stroke on a stairwell right before my eyes. We went to shul morning and night to say Kaddish prayers for my father.

Life then became harder after my father's death. We ended up losing everything. It wasn't like here in the U.S. when someone dies, you have insurance. When my father died, we began to feel poverty. We had never been very prosperous people, and people would say, "All the Jews are rich," and that would hurt me. I have seen poverty.

Samuel's mother Adele with brother Jakob

Samuel's brother, Jakob David "Busiek" Soldinger

My brother Jakob David, whose nickname was Busiek, was 2 ½ years older than me. He was a high school student, headed to business school. He was active in the Jewish Zionist movement and his dream was to go to Palestine. After hearing the rumors of the atrocities that were soon to occur to the Polish Jews and all men would be killed, Jakob decided not to wait around. In December 1939, he headed east, toward the Soviet-controlled territory, hoping to escape the Nazis. I heard he got on a train in 1941 with friends, heading for the town of Sverdlovsk. According to his friends who survived, he made it as far as Russia when the Germans were walking into Russia in 1942, but I do not know exactly

14

what happened to my brother after that. Supposedly he died somewhere there of typhus. When he left home, I never heard from him again.

My sister Sabina (we called her Sabcia) was four years younger than me. I remember her very well, a delightful little gal.

My mother had difficulties, in and out of the hospital, and never really got well. Through this, Sabina was sent to an orphanage for a while. I use to visit my sister there. When my mother was up to it, she would make ends meet by working as a nurse.

As a young teenager, I remember the political talk about Hitler's rise in Germany and the tensions between Germany and Poland. I had just turned 15 years old the day World War II broke out on September 1, 1939.

THE GERMAN INVASION

In order to understand what happens next, both on an international scale and in the lives of the Soldingers, we should mention a major international and geopolitical event. On August 23, 1939, Nazi Germany and the Soviet Union signed an agreement known as the Molotov-Ribbentrop Pact. On its face, it seemed to be a non-aggression agreement. The Germans and Soviets agreed not to invade or declare war on one another.

However, there was a secret agreement tied to the pact, which was widely known to the Allies after the war concluded in 1945. The secret agreement created German and Soviet spheres of influence, dividing Poland roughly in half, with the German sphere of influence over western Poland and the Soviet sphere over eastern Poland. This secret agreement would help explain the events and how Poland was divided in this agreement.

Little more than a week after signing the Molotov-Ribbentrop Pact, Nazi Germany started World War II by invading Poland on September 1, 1939, using a manufactured incident as an excuse for invasion, claiming Polish forces had shot first. In what would come to be called "blitzkrieg" (German for lightning war), German forces swept east across Poland and went on to invade 11 more countries.

Poland had been anticipating German aggression since about 1936, and had begun building up its defenses. Unfortunately, Poland had miscalculated that the invasion would not come until 1942. It would be fair to say that Poland was caught unprepared, if not downright by surprise.

Though their military consisted of a million soldiers, they were lightly equipped with little heavy armor to fight off the invading German tanks and terrifying Luftwaffe, the largest and most formidable air force in Europe. The Polish soldiers were quickly pushed back by the German onslaught.

On the eastern side of the country, the Soviet Union recognized that the attack was the German signal to engage the secret protocol of the Molotov-Ribbentrop Pact. On September 17, 1939, the Red Army invaded Poland from the east. Publicly, the Soviet Union claimed they were on a mission to protect Poland from the invading Germans. Encountering little resistance, the Red Army swept westward toward the dividing line in the pact. Poland, caught in a powerful vice, capitulated in just 35 days.

By October 6, 1939, Germany ruled over western Poland and the Soviet Union controlled the eastern portion. This would be the way of things until 1941, when Nazi Germany launched a massive assault on the Red Army, pushing them deep into Russia and leaving Poland completely under the control of Germany. Most European Jews lived in countries Nazi Germany would occupy or influence during World War II.

I was 14 years old, playing ball in summer camp. Ribbentrop went to Moscow to make a deal, and everything was shut off immediately. They took us by train from summer camp back to Krakow in total darkness and the war started 10 days later.

On August 31, the Polish radio announced that they would be testing sirens in case of an air raid, like a mock-war exercise. We were told to keep our windows covered with black shades and we should all go into our basements or cellars, which still took us by surprise.

On September 1, 1939, I remember that very day the war broke out, when 2 million Germans invaded Poland, marking the beginning of World War II. The German invasion and policies that followed uprooted and destroyed a centuries-old, peaceful way of life in Krakow. Bombs were coming down the very first day, so there was need for the air raid sirens after all. They destroyed a few buildings, but Krakow was not destroyed at all. That was the beginning.

German troops marched in a few days later, with almost no resistance. Big and powerful, they started doing their tricks. The Germans were very much against the Hasidic Jews and began cutting their pais (sideburns) and beards. They tortured them by putting them in front of trucks and made them run for their lives, as a form of cruel entertainment. Some killings occurred. I was just a child, so I was not physically involved like they were.

By September 6, 1939, all Jewish businesses were marked with a large Star of David and business owners had no choice. All the citizens were required to have registration cards and the authorities placed a yellow stripe on the cards belonging to Jews. Upon identification, German soldiers and Polish civilians began looting Jewish stores. Most of the buildings were lit with petroleum, so when the vandalism and theft began, the broken light fixtures leaked petroleum onto everything. The German soldiers sabotaged the food supply with mixing in kerosene. I remember the smell of petroleum hanging in the air.

Beginning October 26, 1939, Hans Frank became the Governor-General of Krakow and the occupied Polish territories. Jews were ordered to forced labor and they started catching us, grabbing us, and putting us on trucks. As a child, I didn't walk the streets, because I felt very vulnerable. One day, a German grabbed me and put me in a truck. We went five… six… seven miles. We then loaded a box of coal. There must have been 20 of us and they grabbed my ID. You are helpless without your ID. I managed to get it back.

Then the soldier calls my name "Samuel Soldinger!" You would not believe it. Another Samuel Soldinger walked out. Someone I did not know. I tried to talk to him. He was much stronger than I was. He was not very happy because he had to work for free and he wasn't very cordial. I never met him before and I never saw him again.

I had worked all day, full of dirt from digging ditches. When the work was finished, I was forced to walk miles back to my neighborhood.

They continued to catch us on the street. On November 28, 1939, a Jewish advisory council called Judenrat was created by the Nazis as a means for dealings between the government and the Jewish community. With its offices in Krakow, it was formed by some very fine Jewish people, such as lawyers and doctors, who tried to help all Jews as much as they could. The Jewish Council made a deal with the Germans: do not grab people off the street. Tell us what you want, and we will get the people for you. If you wanted the freedom to be on the streets, you had to pay the Jewish Council. Some people paid Judenrat to hire other Jewish people to take their place in the labor gangs, although this did not relieve the snatching of people off the streets.

I remember December 1, 1939, as that was the day I began wearing a Jewish star. Anyone 10 years and older had to do so. Then on December 5, 1939, hundreds of German SS troops and police blockaded the Jewish section, the Kazimierz District, where probably 80 percent of the Jews in Krakow lived. The purpose was to confiscate the diamonds, gold, silver and anything of value. They took whatever they desired and it was just plain thievery. Women would be made to strip and walk around nude and many times were raped. Only Polish people who lived there were able to go in and out for two days while this confiscation took place.

As the looting continued in the city, the four to six Germans arrived at our home to do the same. We didn't have anything and they stayed for hours. My uncle Baruch Sherman from Germany was living with us, and an SS officer immediately spotted my uncle's stamp collection and started to flip through it. Suddenly, he ordered all of his soldiers out of our house. When they were gone, he asked my uncle how much would it cost to buy a certain stamp? He bought a single stamp when he could have confiscated the entire collection. They were just crazy, fanatical and inconsistent. It is amazing how all of the sudden this SS became a gentleman and forgot he was dealing with a Jew, just because he saw some stamps. He even thanked my uncle on the way out.

The invasion became even more real to me the next day, when I experienced something awful for the first time: the SS shot at me. This would be the first of many times I would be in mortal danger. On this particular morning, I stepped out of the back of the house into our community courtyard and all of the sudden, shells were fired at me from the rooftops with no warning and for no reason. The SS had stationed themselves from up above and began firing as I ran then through the garden. Of course, I was just a child. I jumped into our neighbor's house, Sam and Sigmund Rotter's, and took shelter there for two days, not daring to venture out. Beginning November 20, 1939, all Jewish bank accounts and safe deposit boxes were frozen and controlled by the Germans. Jewelry, gold and silver became currencies of exchange and the Gestapo took the frozen money.

As the institutional oppression continued, beginning December 11, 1939, the curfew was set for 9 a.m. to 5 p.m. for Jews and only those with special permits were allowed on the street. We did not have a permit. To get one, we had to work for the Germans.

When I was 15 1/2, I worked for them. I would make some money for my mother. I worked for the SS, for the police and for the pilots. I knew them from the beginning and had a lot of experience on who was who and I learned something from them. There were good ones and bad ones. Most of them were fighting the war. The toughest job was working for the SS. Some of them would mind their own business. We cleaned up guns.

I liked the German police the best. They were not SS and were volunteers. I would walk with them and they would send me to buy beer. It was a way of life for me. I went to work. I wasn't hungry. They always gave me some cookies and some bread, which at the beginning of the war was scarce. You name it. I did what I had to do. I cleaned rooms. I washed floors. I didn't know them by name, but they called me Samuel most of the time.

By December 1939, there were 68,482 registered Jews in Krakow, and only a small percentage survived. Jews were barred from public schools and Governor-General Frank gave an order that Jews would have to look out for their own education. This forced the Judenrat to organize private, Jewish-only schools with no outside financial assistance, and my school became obsolete. By January 1940, Jews were not allowed to change residences or move to different villages or towns, and we had to list all of our property. We couldn't have cameras or radios and were not allowed to use public transportation. The non-Jewish Polish people were not allowed radios either.

CHRONOLOGY 1939
Krakow, Poland

9/1/39   War Declared – Immediate Persecution

9/8/39   All Jewish owned stores, restaurants, etc. have to be marked with large, yellow Star of David.

10/10/39 All Jews have to report their residence on special forms marked with a yellow stripe.

10/26/39 Orders by Governor-General Hans Frank forbidding slaughter of animals for kosher foods.

10/26/39 By order of Governor-General Frank, Jews are ordered to do forced labor "Zwangsarbeiter Trupps" (forced labor squad).

10/26/39 Governor-General Frank proclaims that all Jewish exploiters will have no place on his territory. All kosher practices suspended on order of Frank. This day also marked the long process of forcing Jews into slave labor.

11/8/39   From November 8 until November 24, by order of Gestapo, Jews must register at all Government Territory. Final Count by December 29, 1939 was 68,482 Jews.

11/12/39 Jews have to immediately report to authorities, any changes of address and they are forbidden to use streets, roads and marked places from 9:00 p.m. to 5:00 a.m. without a special permit.

11/20/39   Checking, savings accounts and safety deposit boxes in all banks, belonging to Jews, are frozen.

11/23/39   Governor-General Frank freezes (disallows) all privileges to Jewish owned businesses.

11/27/39   All Jewish owned automobiles, trucks and motorcycles have to be submitted to authorities.

11/28/39   Governor-General Frank orders establishment of Jewish Council (Judenrat) to represent Jewish people.

12/1/39   As of 12/1/39, all Jewish men, women and children 10 years of age and older are ordered to wear armbands with the Star of David.

12/5-12/39 A blockade of Jewish district in Krakow called Kazimierz is set up to confiscate gold and silver.

12/9/39   All pensions of military and civil employees and their widows are revoked.

12/12/39   By order of the German School Authority, all Jewish students and teachers are removed forever from all public schools, high schools, etc. All Jewish schools are closed.

12/12/39   SS and police order all Jews 14-60 years of age, to do forced labor for a period of 2 years or longer, and the Jews were placed accordingly with professions into labor camps.

IN THE GHETTO

It was 1940 and Hans Frank was the Governor-General of the occupied Polish territories. The general government was established in the Wawel Royal Castle in Krakow. Krakow was a historical city, with a big, beautiful castle and churches right in the middle of town. In his castle, Frank said he wanted to dispose of 85 percent of the Jews out of Krakow, while the other 15 percent of our people were important for the city. They gave us two or three months to leave Krakow voluntarily. Can you imagine someone asking you to pack your bags, simply because they don't want you there? We could take anything we had with us, up to 25 kilos (55 pounds), so we sold everything we could, like wedding bands. My mother had a little diamond and that was what we lived on. We were lucky we had that. We had to abandon our home and leave everything behind, just carrying a couple of suitcases. Once our entire apartment building was emptied, we were marched by the Poles outside to be bathed and disinfected for bed bugs. Some of the Polish people in charge of this exercise were anti-Semitic.

They wanted control over us. We all wore Jewish stars. Anyone 10 years and older wore a white armband with a Star of David. In some other cities, people had a yellow star on their lapel, but not in my hometown.

My mother decided we would go to Warsaw. She was a poor, sick widow, but maybe she could get a job as a nurse and earn a living to provide for us. I was barely 16, but maybe I could get a job as an upholsterer and we had my younger sister to care for. When we arrived in Warsaw, the entrances were marked with German signs that read "Entrance Forbidden, Territory Endangered by Typhus." We stayed for a few days with acquaintances of mother. They were not very happy we were there. We got a furnished apartment on the 5th floor that had a terrace and the rent was exorbitant. Many of my friends and their parents went to Warsaw, so at least I had a whole gang there.

A German official supervises a deportation action in the Krakow Ghetto. Jews, assembled in a courtyard with their bundles, await further instructions *[C. 1942, United States Holocaust Memorial Museumn/ Archiwum Panstwowew Krakowie, Washington, D.C.]*

In all, it was a disastrous move for us. There were no jobs for my mother, no jobs for me. Whatever my mother had to spend was from the furniture we sold before we left Krakow. We were spending and spending and spending and there was no future there. She was suffering, and still, she went from village to village selling margarine to try to make some money.

It was November 1940 and we had been in the Warsaw Ghetto about three months. The conditions were getting worse and deteriorating day by day. The people were hungry and helpless, walking around like corpses in the streets, falling all around. I didn't witness any punishments in the ghetto, only starvation.

We ate mostly vegetables, potatoes and lots of beans. Occasionally, in the beginning, I would go buy some meat, if we had extra money. I don't think I was hungry. My mother tried hard and we had enough. We didn't have fabulous food, but we ate. To get a loaf of bread, I would stand all night at the bakery window, and still, there was no bread. That wasn't so bad in comparison to what would happen later on. For some people, it was absolutely terrible.

My mother then got inside information that the Germans were closing in on the Warsaw Ghetto. We were not allowed on a train at that point, so with the last money we had, my mother bought a pass. It was probably a fake pass. If we had walked, it would have taken us a week or two, which was about 200 miles. She paid for the forged papers and we left Warsaw by train just days before the Warsaw Ghetto was sealed.

We returned to a village among the farmers named Tonie near Krakow, where the Jews were permitted to go at the time. We could not have gone freely just anywhere. It was ironic, because the village was only about a half a mile from the city. We squeezed into a little room and lived with an older cousin, where we slept in the kitchen. There was a family with a little synagogue in one of the houses next door, where we attended religious services in the basement. I also began to study English. It was marvelous in comparison to the Warsaw Ghetto, although life was much more difficult than our lives in the Krakow we knew before.

After arriving in Tonie, I volunteered to work for Wilhelm Riedel and Son at Rakowice military airport in order to help my mother, which paid a little salary, gave me protection, relatively good food and a special work pass. This pass was a picture ID with a German eagle and it was incredibly valuable, because it allowed me to move throughout Krakow and nearby villages or cities. I worried every time I was stopped, as I also did some photography on the side, taking pictures for IDs, even though it was illegal.

The airport was a private army airport used by Luftwaffe that hired heavy construction laborers and paid us wages and a big bonus of a loaf of bread each week. I walked an hour and a half each way to work, mostly through agricultural areas, and in the rain or snow, as there was no transportation. It wasn't torture, but I worked very hard and was happy to bring something home for my mother and some small wages. I mixed cement and carried a 50-bag quota of cement or coal on my back. I was young and strong and didn't mind. I dug trenches for electrical conduit, climbed tall poles to mount wires and did a lot of electrical installations. I was thinking, as long as I am a good worker, they will keep me. My goal at that point wasn't to help the enemy, but to save our lives. I was optimistic and kept thinking, "The war will be over soon. It has to be over soon."

In the meantime, I used my special work pass to move about the "black market" to obtain milk, bread, chickens and other food I smuggled into the ghetto. Sometimes, I bought and sold goods with the Polish farmers who would lurk in the doorways to sell their wares. Once, a police officer arrested me for possessing milk illegally, so my mother had to come to the German police station and pay a large fine, which was the last of her money at the time.

There was an organized resistance at that point, by the famous Militaria, but I didn't know about it.

In the next step, they built the Krakow Ghetto in Podgorze, across the river from the Kazimierz District. Hans Frank believed that Kazimierz was a more important section of the city and wanted to remove the Jewish community from this district entirely. The deadline was March 20, 1941 for Jews in the villages to report to this newly formed ghetto, which had previously been home to approximately 3,500 people. Now, some 15,000 Jews were being forced to this area where there were only 320 buildings. People were crammed into apartments where each person was allotted two square meters. This meant that as many as four families would share an apartment and diseases like typhus spread like wildfire. I was very lucky that I managed to work at the airport, because by the time they opened this ghetto, I had an occupation, since I was a laborer.

Forced laborers constructing the wall around the Krakow Ghetto. *[1941, United States Holocaust Memorial Museum/Instytut Pamieci Narodowej, Washington, D.C.]*

There was some freedom in the ghettos, as we were allowed to move around a little, but we were not allowed to go to movie theaters, own an automobile or ride on streetcars. The plan and purpose of the ghettos was to corral the Jews. The Germans forced the Jewish residents of the ghetto to build a wall surrounding it and brick off any windows facing the outside. The walls were shaped like tombstones, maybe to remind us of a fate that would lie ahead. We survived day to day, until the killings began in 1942.

A column of Jews march with bundles down a main street in Krakow during the liquidation of the ghetto. SS guards oversee the deportation. *[March 1943, United States Holocaust Memorial Museum/Instytut Pamieci Narodowej, Washington, D.C.]*

March 13, 1943, the Nazis liquidated the Krakow Ghetto, led by Amon Goeth, the SS commandant from Plaszow who was in charge. This took place while I was at the airport. All able-bodied workers were sent to the Plaszow labor camp. Everyone else was murdered. Four thousand Jews: the sick, the old and even children were executed by firing squads. An eyewitness told me he saw children hurled from windows to their deaths.

A section of the Plaszow concentration camp. *[1943-1944, United States Holocaust Memorial Museum/Leopold Page Photographic Collection, Washington, D.C.]*

Plaszow was designated as a labor camp, made up of mostly Jews. The prisoners lived in cramped barracks on meager rations, usually 300 to 400 calories per day. The food was bad bread, which only became worse as the war dragged on, and thin soup, sometimes made from grass. The camp, in a cruel and intentional twist, was built on top of two Jewish cemeteries, which were destroyed to make way for the camp. At its height, Plaszow held 25,000 prisoners.

Hans Frank was executed by hanging after being convicted of war crimes at the Nuremberg trials.

CHRONOLOGY 1940
Krakow, Poland

1/1/40	By order of the SS, Jews are forbidden to move from their present territory and leave Krakow's borders.
1/24/40	Governor-General Frank orders Jews to report all private estates by March 1, 1940.
1/26/40	Jews are not to use the railroads.
3/1/40	Jews are allowed to use streetcars only in trailer cars and specially assigned seats in the rear of the cars.
3/6/40	The Mayor orders all Jews 12-60 years of age, to register for forced labor.
3/7/40	Jews who have medical insurance can only be treated for infectious diseases, etc. in hospitals.
5/1/40	Jews are not allowed to be in parks and main marketplace.
11/1/40	Governor-General Frank orders Jewish Council to establish and take care of education in public schools and in trade schools and hire teachers under the jurisdiction of the German School Council.

11/19/40   All signs indicating various professions of
            Jews (doctors, dentists, etc.) must be marked
            with a blue Star of David.

11/25/40   Jews who work in Krakow and hold important
            jobs are allowed to remain in Krakow with a
            work permit. All other Jews have to report
            with 25 kg (55 lb) or less of baggage to be
            deported. Governor-General Frank declares
            Krakow judenrein (free of Jews).

11/27/40   Jews could only employ non-Jewish
            household help if they had a special permit.

THE POLICEMAN

This is a very unusual story. While most of my stories are very unusual, this one in particular is extremely coincidental regarding a policeman.

In 1940, I was living in a village near Krakow called Tonie. We were not allowed to live in the city and this is where we settled with some of our family after our return from the Warsaw Ghetto. I wanted to make some money and I was always interested in photography, even before the war. I didn't have a camera. We were poor and so I borrowed a camera. In this instance, I borrowed one from some nice people and it was a German brand, a Voigtlander. I started doing business by making pictures, mainly for IDs. One can call it an ID. We called them Kennkarte. Kin-card means, to kin in German, is to recognize a card. A card to recognize.

The Kennkarte was an identity card used in Germany during the Third Reich. They were first introduced in July 1938 and had stamps from the corresponding issuing office and official. Kennkartes were issued to adult male Germans 18 and older, and every male and female Jewish person, who were expected to present the card when confronted by officials.

I went to town. I was allowed to go to town because I had a pass working at the airport. I wore a Jewish star. I was allowed to go to a photo store and buy film. I did not do anything illegally and I bought two rolls of film and photo paper. I remember it like today; there were 12 pictures in each roll.

I walk out of the store and two Polish policemen stopped me to check my pockets. One was an older man, I assume like he was in his 50s, maybe more, and one was quite a young fellow, I'd say in his early 20s. The young fellow was very beautifully dressed with a very beautiful outfit; beautiful shoes and one can call it "dressed to kill."

They spoke with Ukrainian accents from south of Poland, where many of the lumber people lived. They took me inside a back stairway and frisked me. "Take everything out of your pockets." The young one checks that I took out everything, "How much money do you have? What are you doing here? What purpose do you buy film?" Very nasty.

I was just barely 16, and from what I recall, I was crying a little and scared to death. I didn't tell him I am going to do it for business, but I told him I bought the film so I can take pictures and that is not against the law.

It didn't take long when the older policeman realized that I wasn't a good catch. He seemed to be kinder and just stayed more in the background of the young fellow. That is what I assumed. The older man said, "Hey, let him go, he's just a kid." They look at each other, and a few minutes later, they gave me back the film. They did not touch me. They did not beat me. I was just scared. They let me go.

I went back to the village quite upset, of course. I was taking pictures and making a few dollars to help my mother, with this borrowed camera.

Now, it is 1942. In our Krakow Ghetto, there was starvation and problems and lack of food and you name it. To buy food, it was very expensive on the black market, but there was another outlet one could go. Especially me. I had a beautiful pass with a picture because I worked at the German Lufthansa at the airport, so I was allowed to go outside of the ghetto. In some doorways, there were peasants selling eggs, milk, you name it. My mother gave me some money and I took a little can, maybe the size of one quart of milk, so I could carry it under my coat. (One time, I bought a live chicken and hid it under my coat.) In some situations, they were very liberal to allow and the police looked away.

I bought the milk and went out with a can of milk under my coat … and here comes the same young Polish policeman … the same person who stopped me when I had the film.

"You come here! You come with me!" He didn't handcuff me. He didn't beat me. He was just nasty. He took me to a German police station. There, a German man was sitting at a desk in civilian clothes with another guy with a big swastika on his lapel, and both were screaming, yelling and calling me dirty names.

"How dare you to go and buy milk outside, you're not allowed!"

I was helpless. I begged him, "Nothing happened!" He took the milk, took my ID and gives me a little nod, a temporary pass to go back to the ghetto and bring a fine. I cried all the way home and then I brought the fine. I remember it was all the money my mother had - her last 20 zloty - which was an awful lot of money at that time. I was very upset again. No milk, no money and the last 20 dollars my mother had was gone. It was quite upsetting to be in a situation where I didn't succeed to bring that milk home. My mother was a sick woman.

Time passes by and there are many stories that I will tell about survival of the ghetto. My luck of survival took me to Mauthausen, Linz in the small town of Klein Munchen, where I was sent the last few months of the war. One Sunday afternoon probably four to five weeks before the war ended, in April of 1945. I was going to the men's room, the latrine, on a Sunday afternoon. There was one prisoner sitting in the latrine. I came over and he was at the last seat – and there were no other people around. I go about my own business, and all of the sudden, I am looking at this guy and recognizing this policeman, the same policeman. Again. I don't know his name. I never knew his name. The guy is sitting over there in prison garb, very shabby, wrinkled, old and ripped. I could recognize this is one of the prisoners who spent some time in Auschwitz, because he had narrow stripes on his uniform and we had quite a few people, specifically Poles who wore this kind of a uniform. I was almost in shock. A guy like that here, I would say probably 300 to 400 miles from Krakow, another country, and I am seeing this guy again. What should I do? Should I go and call people? Maybe we should kill him, which wouldn't be much of a crime, you know. I could have killed him and no one would know if he was murdered. I didn't have the energy and I didn't think he deserved to be killed. That was something normal. If you killed someone, there wasn't much trouble not to be prosecuted.

After a few moments I said, "Well, if he's a prisoner, so he already paid his debt. The way he wore his uniform, he must have paid his debt.

I just figured I will approach him and simply asked. "Do you remember me?" He looked at me with a very unfriendly, mad face. He didn't seem to be upset at all. Nonchalant, he said, "Well, I don't remember you, but whoever you think I am, I am. I am the Polish policeman from Krakow. I was in Krakow and I was a good guy and I was in Auschwitz and now I am here, as I've been in a concentration camp."

I was speechless. I did not want to add insult to injury and I told him, he had been very mean to me, and on two occasions, unnecessarily. I just didn't have the heart to tell him, "Glad you are here."

I walked out. I hid behind the barrier; I was waiting to see where he was going, where he stayed, to kind of spy on him. I followed him from Block #5 or #6. I was in prison on Block #5 and he went to Block #10. I assumed that is where he lived. I went back to the barrack, I told some of the guys, we had mostly Russians and Ukrainians, and I told them the story. One of them was kind of a sophisticated Polish Ukrainian who I lived with in the barrack. He said, did he look like so-and-so? I said, "Yes." He said, "You know, that's the guy who arrested me. Where is he? Do you know where he went?" I decided not to give him away. I felt that it was my duty to society because he didn't kill anybody that I had seen — he acted like he was a policeman on duty. He could have been nicer to me and to other people and he's already paid to society by being a prisoner. I simply said, "I'm sorry, I don't know, he just took off and I lost him in the crowd." I do think they found him and punished him for me, and many others. That was my opinion.

1940, 1942 and 1945: this is the unusual story of the policeman.

CHRONOLOGY 1941

Krakow, Poland

1/1/41   All Jewish men are ordered to clean snow for a period of 12 days, 8 hours each day. Each man is given documentation for their work, and after January 31, 1941, men without documentation will lose their permit to live in Krakow.

1/15/41   All Jews are being issued Kennkartes as identification. These cards give the Germans complete control of the Jews in Krakow.

2/4/41   All Jewish men and women who have a new Kennkarte (ID), must shovel snow in February, March, April and May for 8 days each month.

2/25/41   All present permits to reside in Krakow are not valid as of February 27, 1941, and only Kennkarte holders are allowed to stay and live in Krakow.

3/3/41   Krakow's Ghetto is being established in a designated area, for all Jews to reside for sanitary and security reasons. All Jews must be there by March 20, 1941 and all Aryans must leave by the same date.

3/15/41   Jews need a special permit to use streetcars.

4/28/41   Kennkartes must be yellow in color with the letter J on the cover. J=Jude, Jude=Jew

10/15/41	Jews who leave the ghetto without authorization will face the death penalty as ordered by Governor-General Frank.
11/12/41	2000 Jews are deported to Lublin, Poland.
11/30/41	Jews are not allowed to sell or give away, gold, diamonds and silver.
12/1/41	The Polish post office does not accept parcels by Jewish senders because of sanitary reasons (may create health hazard and epidemic).
12/27/41	Jews have to give up all furs.
12/31/41	Governor-General Frank orders Jews and Poles to give up skis and ski boots.

THE UPHOLSTERY SHOP

After the invasion and me doing odd jobs, my mother tried to find me an occupation. She said, "You know, there is a man, Mr. Finkelstein, and he is an upholsterer." He was Jewish and I became his helper and I learned very quickly. The upholstery shop was converted from an old movie theater on the prominent Straszewskiego Street and we were in the back of the building.

Mr. Finkelstein was kind of a strange man. He said if I did not impress the owner of this store – who was a half-Polish, half-German woman named Wasilewska – I would lose my job. She was the wife of a judge and her store was only for Germans. One day, he decided to impress the owner and made me make swastikas on the backs of the chairs and put them in the store window. However, it ended up being a sign of disrespect to the Germans, where sitting on or leaning against swastikas was forbidden.

The next morning, the Gestapo came screaming, asking Finkelstein and me about the chairs. It was a terrifying experience. We worried we would be arrested if they found out we were Jewish. Mr. Finkelstein was so scared, he left immediately, never to return. The owner dismissed me and I ran away, up to the roof. She did end up rehiring me, as I was cheap labor.

One day, the manager and I had to open the shop and had no key. Mrs. Wasilewska came to help us unlock the door, irritated, spewing anti-Semitic remarks about the Jews. It was a horrible situation and I was right there. She said, "It was time for the Germans to take care of the Jews, who had dominated the Poles. It was time for the Jews to suffer. They should have been sent to Madagascar a long time ago."Apparently, she was "Volksdeutsche," because she was a Pole who converted as a German and to German ways after the invasion.

I will never forget that. I continued working there nonetheless, and she continued to hire more people. Mrs. Wasilewska then took a job redecorating the Gestapo theater next to their headquarters on Pomorska Street and I became a delivery boy. I would run errands to bring whatever materials were necessary, blocks and blocks, back and forth.

One day, a Gestapo asked me for my ID. I had a Jewish star, but I also had a pass because there was a curfew and I needed a pass to get home after work. The Gestapo was furious when they noticed I was a Jew. Mrs. Wasilewska came running, screaming, "You better go away! Go! They saw your pass and saw Samuel Soldinger. Only Jews are named Samuel and the Gestapo does not want a Jew working here! It would be a disgrace!" She gave me some money and that was the end of my job.

Volksdeutsche was a Nazi term meaning "German folk" referring to ethnic Germans living outside of Germany. After the Germans occupied Poland in 1939, they established a bureau where they registered Polish citizens of German origin as Volksdeutsche. Those who registered were given benefits, including better food and special status. They were given housing, farms, furniture and clothing, all stolen from the Jewish and Polish people sent to Nazi camps. In 1940, the Nazis divided the Volksdeutsche into four categories: ethnic Germans who supported the Third Reich, other ethnic Germans, Polish who had German ancestors and Polish who were related to Germans.

DEPORTATION AND GOODBYES

The Nazis carried out periodic deportations in the ghettos. Those unlucky enough to be selected for deportation faced an almost certain death. Most of the time, those deported were loaded up onto train cars and shipped to Auschwitz or another death camp. Sometimes, upon their arrival in a camp, the Nazis would force the condemned prisoners to write a postcard saying they were safe and being treated well. The postcards were mailed back to the people still living in the ghetto. The deportations were violent, with beatings and shootings. Many people were murdered before they even made it to the trains.

A member of the German SS supervises the boarding of Jews onto trains during a deportation action in the Krakow Ghetto. *[C. 1941-1942, United States Holocaust Memorial Museum/Archiwum Dokumentacji Mechanicznej, Washington, D.C.]*

It was June 2, 1942. They put us together in the ghetto and it was the "Final Solution."

The day before, the Germans put up posters and placards that said tomorrow we would have to register and report to the Gestapo. The passes that we had to leave the ghetto would no longer be valid. The location was at a bank, ironically on the main street in Freedom Square, or "Plac Zgody" and the SS were waiting. It was just like in the movie "Schindler's List." Those employed outside the ghetto would require a new pass marked with a blue stamp. If you brought a pass or had a stamp on your card, you were allowed to stay in the ghetto. If you didn't have a stamp, you had to leave with 25 kilos to this freedom place nearby for the first deportation. This would be my first experience being very close to death.

Tadeusz Pankiewicz in his Krakow pharmacy, circa 1941

The next morning, I was depressed, as I may not possibly get a stamp because I work at the airport. My mother had no occupation and did not qualify. I went and there was a very big line in front of the bank. Unbelievably, my first cousin Ignatz Presser (who was five days younger, than me and worked with me for Wilhelm Riedel at the airport) was lining up and said, "Sam! Sam! Sam!" I said, "Ignatz, what are you doing up there? Why are you always first? Come on. We will go together. Don't rush." He shrugged his shoulders. He didn't get a stamp. Why did he not get a stamp? He worked with me and maybe they didn't recognize him? He didn't speak German and maybe he didn't answer the questions correctly? On the other hand, maybe they didn't like him? Who knows? They took him right away and that is the last time I ever saw him.

At that time, they allowed wives to stay with the husbands. There was no other time they did that. I took my mother's card; she was 46, and I was 17. I put ours together. Maybe I will fold them. Maybe that will work. I thought I could pass her as my wife.

We began to see we were losing people and they were not approving our airport jobs. We thought we might be considered "important" since we worked for a private company. Someone called one of the officials from the legal company. He looked like Schindler, a very handsome man. Half German, and a nice man, from what I could tell. He took our cards and went inside the bank. He came back and they called our names. "Samuel Soldinger" and I opened the card. My card is stamped. That means I am alive. My sister was listed as a minor on my mother's card. My mother's card was also stamped. My mother's was crossed out after all with very heavy chalk that read, "Gestrichen," meaning, "Cancelled." They noticed. That was a tragic day. One of the most tragic days for me, in spite of all of the terrible things I would later endure. Ever since, I have been by myself. Well, I had no choice. It began a terrible life for me.

My mother and sister's deportations occurred three days later. The last moment my mother and I saw each other, I saw her through a garden on a balcony of the apartment where she lived. My mother cried and we said goodbye. When I saw her earlier, she had given me $35 in American money. She knew she would not need the money, but I would. That was all she had and it was very helpful for me.

Like in the movie "Schindler's List," my mother and sister had to line up with baggage and be deported. I saw them going over the bridge with all of those people and I could not stop crying. My mother and sister were deported from the ghetto and then perished in Belzec, a Nazi extermination camp.

I was then saying goodbye to my mother's youngest brother Mietek, my uncle. He had a young baby, was very handsome like Frank Sinatra and was a wonderful man. He gave me a fountain pen as a present.

Arthur Rosenzweig was one of the heads of the Judenrat advisory council, and the Nazis ordered him to supply a list of people to be deported. He put himself and his family on the list, to spare other families. The Germans exterminated Rosenzweig and his family also at Belzec. He was a true hero.

A week passed and it was a Sunday, and they closed the ghetto again. I could not call anybody from the airport, because it was closed. So I went to the bank by myself, lined up, and I was lucky.

Now, the blue stamps were no longer valid and they were issuing blue cards, which was a glued piece of blue paper to my Kennkarte. Unlike the "Schindler's List" black and white movie, it was a blue card. If you did not have this blue card, you would be deported to Belzec and gassed. Basically, you're dead. This friendly Gestapo must have had some kind of sympathy for me that he didn't punish me for previously trying to cheat for my mother. Cheating was normal. You had to cheat to survive. He gave me a blue card. I was safe. The fact I survived this incident was pure luck. My favorite uncle Mietek Presser, his wife Erna and their baby Johan were not so lucky. They did not get a blue card and were deported the same day.

As a survivor, I went back to work at the airport. On the way to the trains, they were shooting at people on the street, just leaving them there. There was a special group and they called themselves "SS Army for the Destruction of Jews," commanded by a vicious Major Von Malottke, and they surrounded the ghetto. They deported and murdered I don't know how many people. That is when I realized they will kill us all, eventually, if they can be that cruel.

I was set to go to work at the airport and it happened that particular day I was assigned to the garage dump. I was with a friend of mine. We were both in the same situation, both crying with loss and with dust and dirt on our faces. I will never forget that day. Then we came back to the ghetto and they were taking people off the streets. They walked them to the train and behind them was a battalion of horses.

The man in charge – the known killer – was Von Malottke. I never met him. Never saw him. He was a high-ranking SS. He and his thugs kept going behind people as they were walking and killing them along the way. The streets were filled with blood that seemed to endlessly trickle and flow down, like rain on the pavement. They followed all of the deportees to the trains, killing many along the two-mile walk. That was the message: they were going to kill us all.

I was there for the second deportation and I pulled through. Mrs. Beitz and her son who I lived with, also got deported. I was now all by myself, in a little apartment and my uncle came to stay with me for a while. He was working somewhere and stole some potatoes. The Polish police came and arrested him in my presence. That was the last time I saw him. Supposedly, he was executed for stealing the potatoes. It was very tragic.

It was quite a terrible life, because there was nothing and no one left in the ghetto for me. On October 28, 1942, that was the third deportation. I got up in the morning and there was no announcement, yet all kinds of commotion in the city, with the SS and police surrounding us. The police said, "Line up wherever you work for." I lined up at the sign of the airport, "Flugplatz," where I belong, at the beginning of the line. Behind me was a balance of people who worked in the area, but different departments. There were about 1,600 people total. From the 1,600 people working at the airport, only 160 survived the war.

This is one of the miracles, believe me. We were standing over there for several hours. There was lots of commotion and we didn't know what was going on. There weren't any stamps. It was a selection process. If you go to the right, you survive; if you go to the left, you die.

We asked the Jewish police and they said, "Don't worry." They were nice and tried to encourage us. There were no beatings. We were on a street called Jozefinska and there was an exit gate to this place my mother was deported. That is where they started to select us and release us. All of the sudden, they told us, "Everyone turn around." I think the Almighty was with me. I was no longer at the beginning of the line, but now I was at the end of line. Something tells me, I do not want to be at the end of the line, but I don't want to go ahead. If we had marched and lined up in four's, I would not be here. It was like 2 ½ blocks to go to the other gate that was on Bochenska Street and everybody ran – approximately 1,600 of us. Being younger, I was faster than the others. By the time I started running, not walking, I was right in the middle of the pack, no longer at the beginning or end. If I had walked, I certainly wouldn't be here to tell about it.

The people who were with me were shorter, so I stood out. A fellow by the name of Wilhelm Kunde (he is depicted in the movie "Schindler's List" as kind of a short guy) was segregating. "Left, right, left, right," he said sternly and arbitrarily, based on our looks, our age and his whim. Then he came up to me with a whip. He just touched me and said "You. Go to the right." Then I heard him say, "We have enough. Everybody else goes to the left." It was luck of the draw, so to speak, whether you survived. Whoever went left was doomed to the gas chamber. They went through a doorway to a big yard and perished. Whoever went right, went outside to the ghetto and lived. My friend and the people next to me all went left. Either I was the last one or next to the last one they let through. Everybody else went to death.

I was thinking somebody was going to put me against a wall and kill me. Of the 1,600 of us, they killed 1,000, including some of my best friends and best workers. For the rest of some 600 of us who got to go to the right, we walked outside the ghetto, without any guards. We were allowed to go into the city. We had passes. We walked into the middle of the gutter and the Polish police were looking at us, staring at us. The police asked us if we were liberated, and we said, "No, we are alive."

CHRONOLOGY 1942-1943
Krakow, Poland

1/5/42   All rules by Governor-General Frank regarding conditions of wages to Poles, rule out the Jews.

6/1 - 8/42   Gestapo are issuing blue cards as permits to reside in the ghetto. Jews are being deported by the thousands in three transports to gas chambers at Belzec. Killings on the streets of the ghetto begins.

7/30-31/42   Gestapo inspect all work permits in order to control who stays in Krakow.

Samuel's mother Adele and sister Sabina were both taken to Belzec Extermination Camp and killed there.

10/28/42   Jews are being picked individually and taken from their homes to be sent to Auschwitz.

11/42   The ghetto is being diminished by size.

12/42   The ghetto is being divided. A - for people employed and B - for unemployed.

3/13/43   The ghetto is being liquidated. All employed are sent to concentration death camp Plaszow and all others (4000 sick, old and children) are executed on the streets of the Krakow Ghetto. Amon Goeth is in charge of the liquidation.

Shoah – /'SHōə/ *noun*

The mass murder of Jewish people under the German Nazi regime during the period of 1941-1945; the Holocaust. Modern Hebrew meaning catastrophe.

Merriam-Webster Dictionary

THE AIRPORT
VOLUNTEER TO PRISONER

After the deportation selections, we got back to the airport and right away they said we couldn't go back to the ghetto. "We need you here to work." They put us in an old bunker near the Luftwaffe base and spread sacks of straw on the cold ground. We spent a couple of nights in the bunker and two days later, they started building barracks. Some other groups came and they built four satellite camps for the remaining people. They did not trust us to be together.

I had been at the airport before because of my volunteer work. Now, there were different people here – the Gestapo – and I became a prisoner. I was no longer an employee of Riedel and had no wages. To be clear, I was not a prisoner in the sense of someone sent to a concentration camp. At that point, they called this a labor camp, yet we were not allowed to leave. I continued working at night and the guards watched us. At least we were fed quite well, with decent soup and a piece of bread. We weren't persecuted. It was paradise compared to the ghetto or the future camps I would endure. The German air force people did not seem to share the same ideals as the Gestapo, so being at the airport wasn't that brutal. From the time I volunteered to my time in forced labor, in all, I worked there about two years.

I remember the time a pilot offered to drop me over France as I was helping him turn his propeller. I declined, which felt like a huge mistake. However, escapees were dealt with harshly. We helped my friend Joseph Shoenberg escape by going over a wire fence without cutting it. Later, a young pilot told us he was found and beaten by the Gestapo, then executed.

We worked outside and even played soccer on Sundays. How it all started was in the evenings, on Sundays, we didn't have much to do. So one of the guys said, "Let's play soccer." We didn't have a ball, so we made a ball out of cork. One day, the one who was in charge of our labor camp – who looked like the worst Gestapo – he told the Jewish policeman, "I didn't say they can play ball." The next day, they found a way and we got a ball shipped in. We played and had soccer matches, camp against camp. One side was the prisoners, and the other side was soldiers, with a German referee, and we had professional players among us. Hundreds of people came to watch us. The referee even sent a guard around the field to ensure nothing disrupted play. Even though many were indoctrinated to beat and kill Jews, they enjoyed watching us play soccer. That was our Sunday entertainment. That part was wonderful and that went on for a long time.

We were in the easiest labor camp jurisdiction being at the airport. However, a few months later, the SS started creeping in and coming more often from Plaszow. They resented we were still at the airport. Plaszow was in another area nearby and we kept hearing horrible rumors of the hangings of friends and killings, so we were lucky to be at the airport. Yet the rumors kept coming that we too were going to liquidate and head to Plaszow where the killer was, Amon Goeth.

Typically, at the airport, even though it was a labor camp, we were roaming around free, and then locked up at night. One day in January 1943, we were sitting on the ground eating soup for lunch. The chief of the Jewish police came over with a bunch of people and surrounded us. Amon Goeth, the killer and commander of Plaszow came over. He had a handsomeness about him and was powerful looking, yet the warts on his face added to his villainous reputation. He was mean. He was intoxicated. He lined us up and said, "Empty your pockets." They confiscated everyone's property: watches, diamonds, gold, cigarette lighters and just about anything of any value. I emptied my pockets with what little I had left from the $35 my mother gave me. Maybe I had $5. Goeth came up to some of us. He came up to me. He didn't ask my name and called me "Fritz." "Did you give everything away, or do you still have something?" he said. I told the truth. "I gave you everything, but back in my barrack, I have a fountain pen from my uncle." Goeth said, "Get in the truck." Then, a group of 20 or 30 of us got in a truck and went to the barracks, which were across from the airport.

Commandant Amon Goeth rides his horse in the Plaszow concentration camp. [*March 1943 – September 1944, United States Holocaust Memorial Museum/Leopold Page Photographic Collection, Washington, D.C. Photographer Raimund Titsch.*]

I went into my jacket pocket and gave my pen to Goeth. It was given to me by my dear Uncle Mietek who was sent to death during one of the selections. The pen was very precious to me, but I was now liberated and a free man from that situation when I gave it to Goeth. I was not vulnerable any more to be murdered or killed, this time, anyway. A friend of mine, Samuel Kopec, didn't give up his plain cigarette lighter and they put him against the wall and nearly executed him, when the German police were in charge. They had a lot of German police helping and my friend said he forgot to give it – and they spared his life at the last minute and let him live. (The last time I spoke to him, he lived to be in his 80s in Bolivia, thank God.)

A couple of weeks later, I look back in my pocket – and would you believe it – the pen was still there! It was a fabulous pen, a Pelikan. I just don't understand, I thought to myself. It was a very popular pen with a green handle. Somebody must have secretly got my pen back and planted it there, or someone had an identical one and wanted me to have it. I am not sure exactly what happened, but I didn't say anything. I took the pen and dumped it in the garbage. I did not want to take a chance, since it was very dangerous.

Usually, Goeth was far away. He had several assistants, one by the name of Leo John. He was short, fat and considered the next in charge. He was very vicious when he would come. He used to beat us and shoot, so while even though we were at the airport, we were not completely free from harm.

Around this time, in February 1943, I ended up contracting rheumatic fever, yet I did not know it. I was sweating, shivering with chills and they put me in an empty bunker, where I laid on empty ammunition boxes on a cement floor without medicine, because there was no hospital. So John comes over, the same time I was there, which was an unbelievable situation. He came into the main area with a doctor, Dr. Rostal, and told the doctor to get in the truck, because they were liquidating the area. I knew this doctor very well. He was a young, good-looking guy and he said, "But who will be the doctor?" They made him get the witnesses, lie down and get undressed. John killed him right away because they did not need him anymore. There was also a young Jewish boy in the room, an assistant to a dentist, someone I knew very well. He was ill and John killed him in bed. As it turns out, Goeth was nearby. Apparently, he looked at his watch and didn't have time to come across the runway, where I was sick. That is what the police told me. They said he would be sure to come next time.

The next day, my friend said, "Sam, get dressed! Let's go to work!" I said, "I can't even walk." I was shaking. I was so sick. A low-ranking police officer came with a machine gun pulled me back and said, "Where are you going? We don't need sick people here."

"You can't stay here. They will kill you," my friend whispered to me. My friend then grabbed the policeman by the collar, shook him and said, "He's coming with us." My comrades dug a foxhole and covered me with paper sacks while they worked. The Polish foreman, Twarog, looked the other way and pretended not to see. Their actions saved my life. I would have been shot and killed otherwise.

Amon Goeth was a vile man, an SS officer who ran the Plaszow camp. He oversaw the violent liquidation of the Krakow Ghetto and the operation of Plaszow, where an estimated 8,000 people died. He was unusually cruel, even for a high-ranking officer in the SS. A large and physically imposing man, he reveled in violence and murder. Sam referred to him as "The Murderer" or "The Killer." The scene in the movie from "Schindler's List" which depicts him shooting prisoners from his villa was not exaggerated. He had two large dogs he would sick on prisoners on a whim. It was Goeth, a man who rewarded and delighted in violence, who made Plaszow a terror for all prisoners.

THE DAYS OF OSKAR SCHINDLER

While most everyone around him had died, Samuel survived the Holocaust working in Oskar Schindler's factory.

"You, you and you."

At the airport, trucks and guards with guns arrived to remove all the prisoners and take us to Plaszow, which coincided with Amon Goeth's liquidation of the Krakow Ghetto, where thousands of people were shot.

However, I was lucky. Before we were loaded on the trucks at the airport, an SS officer toting a machine gun asked if there were any machinists and many of us stepped up. I volunteered and said I was an electrician and the guard said, "Close enough." He pulled 30 of us out. They took the rest of the other laborers to the camp at Plaszow, and the 30 of us landed at Oskar Schindler's enamelwork factory. There I met my godmother, four cousins and many close friends. It was a wonderful feeling not to have been sent to Plaszow. It was 1943.

We met Schindler immediately. We had never heard of Oskar Schindler or anyone like him. He was dashingly handsome like a movie star, elegantly dressed and wearing a beautiful diamond ring, holding a cigarette. With a kind smile, he came and welcomed us, but did not say anything at first. He just smoked. That was the first time I saw him and I didn't know he was Schindler.

Instead of starting from the right of the line, he started from the left and I was one of the first. At that point, he talked to each one of us, still with a cigarette. He was a chain smoker. He asked if I spoke Czech, because he wanted to be understood, which is very similar to Polish. I did not speak Czech fluently, but I understood it fluently. My grandmother was Czech and she spoke it sometimes.

He said a few words with a smile on his face, and just to look at him, I could tell he could not hurt us. He was a friend. He had a magic way about him. He was a German with a kind face. Yet, I was terrified, as I couldn't believe a German could be so nice and kind.

Schindler asked me what I could do and I told him I have some experience from a technical school. I tried to tell him the truth. He listened to me for a while, then he patted me on the shoulder and said, "Don't worry, don't worry. You will be good here. You shouldn't be afraid." He told us that we were not there to be murdered, but rather to be peacefully occupied, working for him. I was not the only one, as he treated everyone that way. Then he went on to the next one, the next one, and the next. He towered over most people and would lean down to speak with them.

He immediately assigned each of us to barracks, and after that, we had some belongings. I was still sick, because I came in sick from the airport. I was afraid to go to report it to the doctor. That was scary, because you don't know who they are or what they are going to do to you, which could be a mistake.

There were a number of Jewish police officers who kept order at Schindler's plant, and they were generally disliked for their mean spirit. They wore hats reminiscent of the Polish cavalry with wide yellow bands that looked ridiculous. We called them the "Polish Cavalry from Staniewski's Circus." These policemen had their own private rooms and could live with their families. One of the nice ones was a policeman named Offman, who coincidently I knew very well, as he had owned a shoemaker supply store next to our restaurant in Krakow.

The next morning, I was assigned to work by a machine. I spent a few hours learning how to work on a lathe, which wasn't so bad. Then a Polish boss, the foreman, motions for me to come. They put me in a room where they work with sulfuric acids, used to etch pots, but actually, we used them to remove impurities off metal, heating the materials in ovens to soften them. This process was called "annealing" and we were making ammunition parts and artillery shell casing materials. I started making ammunition from the moment I arrived with Schindler. The fumes were just terrible, especially with my poor health.

In working with the acids, Schindler would come visit me occasionally. Yet, it was very difficult for me to breathe there, especially since I was sick and my joints were swelling. A few days later, I reported to the doctor after I collapsed. I was very sick and stayed in the hospital barracks, and finally I saw Dr. Samuel Rubinstein. He was trying to diagnose me, not yet knowing I had rheumatic fever. My fever was very high and he must have been afraid I was contagious. They decided to take me to the hospital in Plaszow, where the killer Amon Goeth ruled the camp. They hired the Jewish policeman, Mr. Offman, and a Ukrainian guard, and with Dr. Rubinstein, we all traveled by horse and carriage. They dismissed the driver long before we got to the entrance. We got out of the buggy and we walked the rest of the way to the Plaszow camp, which was maybe a quarter of a mile.

When we got to the hospital, a fellow dressed in civilian clothes by the name of Zdrojewski met us at the gate and jumped at us because we came especially late in the afternoon. We tried to comingle with people, so no one would see us and be inconspicuous, but he spotted us, as it was a very narrow entrance. He pulled a gun and began screaming and yelling, "We don't need sick people here!"

Finally, Dr. Rubinstein bravely said to the German, "Schindler sent us because he wants Soldinger well. He is a very important worker." Well, that was a lie. I was a teenager. I was no more important than the others were. But it worked. Zdrojewski said, "Oh yes," and I was let through, probably because he expected to be paid with some cognac from Schindler. The Plaszow hospital only had a few blankets and no real medical equipment, and the camp was unbelievable with the killings and hangings. But I made it.

Then Dr. Rubinstein saved my life again. When I was in the hospital, a fellow by the name of Miller, who was the head of a labor camp like Plaszow called Prokocim, came wandering in drunk like a pig and looking to cause trouble. I was being examined by Dr. Rubinstein, Dr. Blassberg and Dr. Hilfstein, who were trying to diagnose my fever. Dr. Rubinstein minimized my condition and sent me away with a couple of aspirin, so I would not get Miller's attention or wrath.

Then Schindler saved me. The doctors called him and it was lucky he was there. At that point, Dr. Rubinstein said, "He has a slight fever and Soldinger is going back to work tomorrow." Miller probably could have killed me and killed the doctors, you never know – or maybe he was trying to scare me? I do not know. The police informed Schindler. He came, completely intoxicated, and I saw him standing at the door, but he did not walk in. He didn't see me, didn't talk to me, but he talked to the Nazis and told them not to touch me, not to kill me. After Schindler came, it was all fine. In the book "Schindler's Legacy," Dr. Rubinstein writes about how Schindler saved me.

I was in the hospital for five days. I was worried I wouldn't be picked up and taken back to Schindler. I was fortunate too, because one of the other doctors, Dr. Weinreb and a nurse named Sulamith had both worked with my mother when she was a nurse. I said, "I am Adele's son." Right away, they saw that I got better and better, and came every day to check on me and made sure I had good blankets. I was lucky. Dr. Weinreb protected me from the vicious person in charge of the hospital in Plaszow, Dr. Leon Gross. He was the most horrible man and mistreated patients. Consequently, he was later executed by the Polish government for war crimes.

After a week, my fever abated and I was taken from the Plaszow hospital and returned to work for Schindler in the factory.

I do not like to talk badly about Schindler, but one day, the Polish foreman named Novak - who was a very nice guy to work for and was a good foreman - fell asleep on the job. I liked him very much and he always had a smile on his face. Novak didn't care if we could get all the work done. However, that night, he made a mistake. Usually, Schindler came at night for inspections. Schindler saw him asleep, and gave him a punch so rattling, Novak flew in the air. I do understand that he deserved it to be an example, as Schindler could not just ignore it.

The next day, a Polish engineer came to assess the workload. He was young and stuck up, a "Volksdeutsche" who had been converted to Nazism. He came to me because I knew what to do there. I had been there about a month, so he made me foreman.

"Mr. Soldinger, you're in charge." I did not open my mouth. Why me? I am only a teenager. Then again, why not me? Actually, I was the only one who was an expert in that room and I knew how to mix the acids.

So I began working and working and trying and trying, but I was a poor performer as a leader, as I was young and people wouldn't listen to me or respect me. My attitude was, I had better do the work, because somebody has to get it done, because I am responsible. Therefore, I did the work of two or three people, and one day, I simply didn't have enough done. They said there was not enough work coming out of the factory and I needed to increase production.

"Mr. Soldinger, do you want to go against the wall?" one of the guards said to me. I knew I could be shot for not making the quota. Then I began pushing my team, and ultimately, I had an argument with a couple of the people who worked for me. They were about seven or eight years older, and kind of laughed it off, that this young guy isn't

going to tell them what to do. They took advantage. I don't
know who started the fight. The guards didn't know either.
They took us in the guardhouse, just as you see in
"Schindler's List," and gave us 10 lashes each. I got very
mad and started making noise. I told them, "I am too young
to be foreman!" I told the engineer the same thing and how
we got the beatings. He said, "Why didn't you tell them you
are a foreman?" I did tell them and it didn't help. So he went
and told the guards not to touch me. Then I went to my
cousin Berek Presser who was a foreman in another part of
the factory and begged him to help me be transferred. The
Nazi engineers ended up hiring a new foreman. After I
trained him, I was reassigned to another part of the factory.

I began working with lathes and presses, which were
tedious and dangerous, and I worked 12-hour shifts. Since
all of our watches were confiscated, we measured time by
one whistle to the next. There were five different presses and
I operated pressing brass rings, which was part of the shell
casings. What made it dangerous, was removing the rings
from the press and I have scars on my hands from the press
slamming down. I ended up getting an infection from one of
these cuts and Dr. Rubinstein had to operate on me without
anesthetic. Many workers lost their fingers. I am fortunate I
only came out with scars.

One day, I was working on a machine and it jammed.
It was a tragic situation, because you cannot buy a new
machine during the war. It was a small part, a fuse, and I
was lucky I didn't lose my fingers because I was trying to
retrieve it without a wrench. Immediately, there was a big
alarm and the engineers came running, two of them who
were Germans. I was desperate and called a crew to help me,
because I would be condemned. Before me, a worker by the
name of Danzinger who lived in my barrack had a die break
off his machine. Even though it was not his fault, the German
engineers called the Gestapo, who picked him up and took
him to the gallows in Plaszow to be executed. When

64

Schindler learned what had happened, he raced to Plaszow, rescued Danzinger, put him in his own car and brought him back.

So when my machine jammed, I was panicked and helpless. When the bell or horn rings, that means it's lunchtime. My co-workers took off for lunch, rather than staying to help me fix it. How could I possibly do this by myself? Someone told me to go to this new building, where they are expanding the factory, and get a jack, just as you would use on your car. Rolling my wheelbarrow, off I went. It was my fortune that the guy in the building happened to be my cousin Berek Presser. He could leave his job because he too was on his lunch break and happened to know this machine inside and out.

Berek said, "Samek, we will do it together." I had the jack and he took a piece of wood and popped it up against the wheel. "I will press from the front and you in the back. When I say, 'One, two, three,' give it a turn until I tell you to stop. Sure enough, we finally got the machine freed and everything came out of the machine with very minor damage. My cousin saved my life for what easily could have been a fatal punishment. I just called him recently (1995) not long after "Schindler's List" came out and I reminded him how he helped me in that situation.

One other day when I was working in the factory, I was near the main door and Schindler came in. Usually, he would come at night, after partying smelling of whiskey. He always smoked and wore that big diamond ring. This time, he came during the day. He came over to me and asked me if I knew how to swim. I said, "Yes, I know how to swim." He was very intoxicated and said, "What would be nice if you could swim the Atlantic Ocean to freedom, because they want to kill you all." He patted me on the shoulder, like he cared.

Another time, I was working late and took two of his round basins, brand new ones, that were about to be shipped out. We were not allowed to, but we did that. So, I put my laundry in a basin, mixed the soap powder, and let it stay there. Schindler comes in and goes behind my legs, behind me, while I am working. He kicks off the lid of one of the pots with his foot to see what is going on. He sees my laundry and pushes it back with his foot. Just like that. He didn't say a word and patted me on the shoulder.

At one point, Schindler was out of town and they took two guys from the camp. One was a young fellow, a distant cousin of mine. He was 16 years old and whistled a Russian song. Somebody reported him and they took him to Plaszow with a young engineer as an example to scare all of us that Schindler didn't have all the power. We should be afraid. They took the young teen to the gallows to be hanged and the rope broke. He tried to beg Amon Goeth not to rehang him, so instead, Goeth shot his feet. In the meantime, the other guy by the name of Krautfiert, someone had given him a razor in his pocket and he cut his wrists, so he fell dead, but they hanged him anyway. They wanted prisoners to have to continue walking by the hanging body and be scared by witnessing it.

When Schindler returned, I watched him save a prisoner by the name of Lamus from being killed by Goeth. Lamus, who was an old farmer from a small village, was sweeping the courtyard in the camp when he should have been in the barracks. He was illiterate, didn't realize the danger, and didn't go for cover. When Goeth arrived with Schindler, Goeth began yelling at Lamus. His assistant, "Hujar" made him lie down, and pulled his gun, prepared to shoot Lamus. Schindler said, "Wait, why shoot this old dog? I'll buy him from you for a bottle of cognac." Goeth spared his life, but still ordered Hujar to give Lamus 50 lashes. Sadly, understandably, Lamus was never the same after that.

On one evening, I was going building to building with a wheelbarrow full of ammunition as part of my duties, and the head of the Gestapo, Julian Scherner, stopped me. He was drunk and picked up a gun. He wasn't pointing it at me.

66

He just held the gun. Still, I thought he was going to try to kill me. You never know with these guys. He said to me, "Come here!" I asked, "Why? Why?" He then asked, "Do you work here?" I said, "Of course, I do the best I can. I am very good. I work hard. I like my work." All this in German. I didn't speak German before the war. He was mad about all of the laughter, the dancing and singing coming from Schindler's parties at the penthouse. Sherner got in my face, started asking questions about Schindler, and finally holstered the gun. He asked me to get Schindler. I ran to the guardhouse, and in German, I called to the driver of Schindler. I knew him, so I told him, this guy wants you and wants Schindler. With a sigh of relief, that was the end of that moment.

There was one camp with barracks, which was predominantly Schindler prisoners, who worked for the Schindler factory. Then there was another group of 200 to 300 people who worked for NKF and they were making and repairing the parts for the airplanes, while another group made wooden boxes owned by Mr. Yaert.

Newe Kuhler Fabrik (NKF) was a factory where refrigerators and aircraft parts were manufactured.

We were all in one yard with all of those barracks. Schindler built the camp because he complained he was losing too much time by people going back and forth. If people can stay there and sleep there, he can save a lot of time. The conditions at Schindler's camp were quite good compared to Plaszow. He provided showers to control the spread of disease. We could bathe once a week and could wash every day, although there was very little soap. I was always dirty because I worked with oil operating the presses and lathes. I only had one pair of pants for months, made out of paper sacks. When some clothes finally arrived, a Jewish chief of police said with laughter that with all of the oil on my pants, they were probably waterproof. Despite the relatively humane conditions, compared to Plaszow, there were reminders that we were still enslaved prisoners. Our shirts and pants were painted with yellow stripes, so we could easily be recognized, if we escaped. We were tattooed. I have the initials "KL" which stands for Konzentrationslager, or concentration camp, tattooed on my left arm by Dr. Rubinstein.

And there were towers. Every two days, there was a change of guards with one SS officer and German police. Unbelievably, they did not walk inside the camp and stayed outside to guard us. I think Schindler kept them that way. He did not want them walking around. In one of those groups, there were Ukrainian guards and they didn't speak German. They were known to be anti-Semitic.

The barracks where we slept was also our synagogue and a number of prisoners in my barrack maintained religious observances continuously, despite the mortal dangers. Rabbi Menasha Lewartow, who slept in the bunk next to mine, led the prayer service every evening. He smuggled in the Torah in a container for water so none of the guards would suspect. I was not particularly religious, but sometimes I joined them in order to make up a "minyan," which traditionally was a group of 10 men needed to conduct certain prayers. One night, we were praying and a German police officer walked in as we were clearly visible, since the barracks lacked any curtains. We were stunned and speechless, although the Torah was not exposed. I thought about how the Germans murdered the Jehovah Witnesses for praying. The policeman said, "You are doing a terrible thing. I won't do anything to you, but you are endangering your lives." He gave us good advice not to do it anymore. He could let us off, because he had no witnesses. He did not want to hurt us. He was a human being.

There were probably a dozen of my best friends before the war and extended family with me at Schindler's factory.

Ben Friedman was my best friend and he was with me. My friend Louis Oppenheim was there, along with his sister. I had cousins there and my godmother was there. As I mentioned earlier, one of my cousins, Berek Presser, was there. He was a foreman on one of the machines. He survived and today (1995) lives in Australia. It was like having one big family there.

As we continued with Schindler, life was quite normal He gave us a soccer ball and he watched us from the rooftop on Sunday afternoons as we played. He also let us listen to the news of the war on BBC Radio. As I have mentioned, he was a chain smoker. He would smoke one or two puffs of a cigarette throw it on the ground so someone could pick it up and have a smoke. He could not have just given away cigarettes, to stay in the good graces of the SS. I watched in amazement as a young woman, about 20, who had never smoked quickly snatched one up and took a huge puff, since it was a cigarette that Schindler had smoked. She picked up the habit in homage to him. While life was hard, it was not as bad as it could have been with Schindler.

When working for Schindler, Sam's rheumatic fever returned. Schindler sent him to the hospital in Plaszow for treatment on a couple of occasions. While Sam was recovering on the last visit, the Russian army got so close to Krakow that Plaszow began to be liquidated. This is when Schindler's famous list was developed. Schindler was able to save 1,200 Jews from Plaszow and have them transferred to his new factory, in what is today's Czech Republic. There they rode out the end of the war. Unfortunately, Sam's name was not on the final list, but his sur name is mentioned in "Schindler's List." It is unknown why, but it is believed this was likely due to his being away at the camp hospital.

Meanwhile, Schindler was building a new factory, a new extension in Krakow, as the Russians were coming closer and closer and the Germans were retreating from Stalingrad. He was planning to go near his hometown in Bruenitch, Czechoslovakia and we were told he was building a factory there. He bought property and we would all go with him.

Like in the movie, he lined us up and said, "Tomorrow, (August 9, 1944) they are allowing me to keep some of you. Unfortunately, I cannot take you all, but you will be in a safe place. As soon as the factory is ready in two or three months, you will be brought back. I have a list and all your names are on that list. I have everything arranged with the Gestapo."

He was apologizing he could not take more of us, which I believed. He said it was only temporary and we would not be separated for long. We were skilled workers and would be doing something more useful, while the equipment was being dismantled, moved and reassembled at the new factory. As soon as the factory was built, he needed us there, so that was quite encouraging. We were happy that he was thinking about us and we were lucky we had him. It was paradise being with Schindler. He protected us. He did his job and he had to be quiet about it, so I do not think he lied to us, yet I don't think he knew himself where we were going. Schindler opened his food warehouse and gave us all cans of pâté, crackers and eggs, etc., to keep us from starving on the journey.

Leaving his factory, I was among the group being sent to Mauthausen and the women went to Auschwitz and Ravensbruck. Most of us men stayed together. We spent the day in Plaszow, where the killer Amon Goeth was. In the evening, they put us in boxcars, just slightly off the railroad track just outside the main gate. It had been a hot day and we spent the whole night there sweltering. There were 120 of us in a wagon, standing room only, with a couple of people who were sick and got to lie down. There was no bread, no food, and no water. Like many others, I mostly stood on one leg. This was the first time I was ever in a boxcar. We did not know what was going to happen or where they were going to take us.

Early the next morning, I was an eyewitness to something unbelievable. Right down Jerusalem Street, Oskar Schindler arrived in a beautiful carriage. He was wearing a beautiful beige suit and a straw Panama hat and was coming to say goodbye to his "children." He stopped the carriage and we all started screaming in German, "Direktor! Direktor!" We had no water. We had no air. We couldn't breathe. He jumped off the carriage and wanted to do something for us, just as a father or mother would. He was an unbelievable prayer answered. He stood there on the steps of the carriage, just like an angel, but his face was frozen and he didn't say anything. He did not know what to do, but he was right by us and was thinking, you could tell. He must have stood there a couple of minutes. He motioned for the driver to go and split the horse, and he went to the gate. He went inside and it did not take long, maybe 20 minutes. He reappeared with soldiers from the camp who brought water and made us get off the train. Unlocking the wagons, boxcar by boxcar, we each got off the train to get a drink. After that, they sprayed the train with water, which actually was not a good idea, because there was too much steam and it became a furnace.

That was the last time I saw Schindler during the war. We all expected to be reunited with him shortly and be under his protection again, but that was not to be. None of us were prepared for what was to follow. We would all now be beyond Schindler's protective influence. The time I spent in Schindler's factory was about a year and a half.

About five or six months after the war, I did see Oskar Schindler in a displaced persons camp in Linz, Austria. He stayed with a fellow named Fettschlein. Oskar was poor and primitively dressed, wearing shabby clothing. He was using Fettschlein's apartment and slept on a cot that was left over from when we got out of the camp. There was an open window and we all went to see him. Schindler was sitting there and we used to go talk to him through the window. As soon as he saw me, he nodded and walked to the window from where he was. I was surprised and flattered that he recognized me. I shook his hands and spoke enough German to say, "Thank you very much. I regret that I couldn't be with you until the end, but you saved me anyway." He said, "I did everything I could." Then I asked him why were we sent to Mauthausen and we didn't get back? I told him it was our problem because some of us were so mad at him. Schindler said, "That wasn't up to me. That was up to Goldberg. Marcel Goldberg was in charge of the list."

Marcel Goldberg was a Jewish clerk assigned to the new Plaszow commandant, Arnold Buscher, who played the largest role in compiling the transport list. There were different lists that emerged over a series of months... and Goldberg collected the diamonds. Goldberg constantly meddled with the list, dropping people and adding others seemingly at random in an effort to ensure his own survival. Perhaps Goldberg's meddling is the reason Sam's name was left off the final list. It could be that Sam was young, alone and at the hospital, and much of the negotiations in creating the list were to keep families together. Without a family, Sam may have been overlooked in the final accounting. Mietek Pemper, the clerk who drafted the actual list, noted that Goldberg's frustrating and underhanded attempts failed, as he was deported to a death camp.

At that point, Schindler lived and spent the rest of his life among us, because that is where he felt most comfortable. He used to stay at my friend Henri's apartment in Munich. Everybody helped him. The benefits were not great, because we were all poor, but he got what he got, whatever we could give to him. In Israel, they were deducting wages from people who volunteered to give part of their salary to Oskar Schindler. We worshipped him. As far as I am concerned, he is the greatest man who ever lived. I give him all the honors.

I also give credit and hold Steven Spielberg in the highest regard for making the movie "Schindler's List." The movie is a Godsend that allowed survivors to come out of the closet and publicly talk about the horror of the Holocaust, supporting human rights. The movie is altered and it is not 100 percent, nor could it be, because it is a movie. It is unbelievable what he did in showing the story and it is a beautiful movie. I think I could have helped him with it.

If someone were to ask me, I would say Schindler was a good man. A marvelous man. In all the time I spent with him, he was like a father to us. He was very gentle. We had a feeling of security being with him. I love him very dearly for all he did for me and especially for all of the people he saved.

Oskar Schindler was born in what is today part of the Czech Republic. He was a man who enjoyed the finer things in life – nice clothes, fast cars, beautiful women, good food and drink. Schindler started secretly working for German intelligence, the Abwehr, in 1936, gathering information on the Czechoslovakian government for Germany. In 1939, he joined the Nazi party. After the invasion of Poland, he moved to Krakow where he acquired an enamelware factory, where he figured he would profit supplying the German army with pots and pans. At its peak, the factory employed more than 1,700 people, the vast majority of whom were Jews.

Sam kept this photo of Schindler in his wallet for the rest of his life.

The entrance to Oskar Schindler's Emalia enamelworks at 4 Lipowa Street in Krakow-Zablocie. [*1943-1944, United States Holocaust Memorial Museum/Leopold Page Photographic Collection, Washington, D.C.*]

Oskar Schindler's enamelware factory during construction.

Oskar Schindler with his horse on the grounds of the Emalia enamelworks in Krakow-Zablocie. *[United States Holocaust Memorial Museum/Leopold Page Photographic Collection, Washington, D.C.]*

Schindler was a man who liked to make money. He did not set out, upon his arrival to Krakow, to save the lives of anyone. However, at some point fairly early in his time in Krakow, the money became a means to saving the lives of people who worked for him.

Schindler used his connections in the Abwehr and his large personal wealth to bribe SS officers and other Nazi officials in order to keep the Jews working in his factory, safe. He would throw lavish parties and shower expensive gifts on the Germans to keep them looking the other way and ignore what he was doing at the enamelware factory. He had to work extremely hard and spend a lot of money to keep a monster of a man like Amon Goeth happy. Somehow, with enough gifts and expensive Schnapps, Schindler managed to do it.

Oskar Schindler at a dinner party in Krakow. At parties like this, Schindler contacted various SS and German officials, which often led to tips about impending deportations that enabled him to save his laborers. *[April 28, 1942, United States Holocaust Memorial Museum/Leopold Page Photographic Collection, Washington, D.C.]*

In the end, the Jewish people returned the favor, helping Schindler to escape from a certain death that awaited him as a member of the Nazi party, had he been captured by the Soviets.

On October 9, 1974, Schindler died penniless, having used his fortune to bribe authorities to save his workers. He is buried at Mount Zion Roman Catholic Franciscan Cemetery in Jerusalem, Israel.

Leaving a stone or pebble of remembrance on a grave is an ancient Jewish tradition with many interpretations. This photo depicts all of the love and admiration people around the world - and the Schindler Jews who survived - have for Oskar Schindler.

AND THEN THERE WAS MAUTHAUSEN

Mauthausen, which operated from 1938 to 1945, was one of the largest, most notorious Nazi concentration camps, along with its network of sub-camps, which included quarries, mines, munitions factories and plant assembly for fighter aircraft. Located on the Danube River near Linz, Austria, Mauthausen was the first and most massive of complexes, where 200,000 prisoners were tortured. While there are no official figures, it is estimated that 120,000 died from starvation, disease and inhumane labor. It was the last to be liberated by the Allies in 1945 and the main camp is now a museum.

After leaving the Schindler factory, the train finally began to move and we found some slight comfort from the little breeze that found its way into our crowded wagon. We traveled a few hours and the train again came to a halt. Looking through the small slats, we could tell we were on railroad tracks next to a very large concentration camp. Later, we would learn it was Auschwitz.

I remember the odd smell that drifted above Auschwitz, as if something had burned. In the distance, I could clearly see the night sky illuminated with some unknown source. This was a horrid place. Only after the war did we learn how truly horrible it was.

We stayed on the train, and we could see barracks, and the guards and the prisoners running about, but no one came to unlock our cars. We thought they would take us in the morning. But they didn't. No one came to get us.

One of the men in our car had smuggled a pair of pliers, which he intended to use to remove the wire from the boxcar window and escape. A former policeman advised us to keep him away from the windows, because if one person escaped, the Germans would certainly punish the entire car.

After waiting overnight in the cars, the train began moving again for another three days and nights, to where we did not know. We were kept on the train - where thirst, hunger and the smell of urine were our constant companions. Men had relieved themselves into food dishes or paper, then threw the excrement through the barbed wire covering of the overhead boxcar windows. We stopped a few times and each time, Dr. Rubinstein managed to get out of his car and go from boxcar to boxcar to help people. He was with his brother and they both wore white doctor coats. The German guards beat them for doing this.

At the final stop, it must have been 4 o'clock in the morning, but none of us could tell for sure. The SS had long ago confiscated all of the Jewish prisoners' watches, along with virtually all of our other possessions.

We heard boots running along the sides of the wagons, with someone fumbling to unlock our car. Suddenly, the door slams open and German SS men scream at us, "Raus, raus Juden! Out, out Jews!" We got off, one boxcar at a time, and the rush of fresh air felt so good, but we had little time to enjoy it. Instead of letting us out to stretch our legs, cramped from being in a cattle wagon, we were greeted with kicks, jabs and blows from rifle butts to our backs. I pushed to the middle of the crowd as far as my aching legs would allow, stumbled, then regained my balance. All SS, nothing but SS beating us and beating us. It was unbelievable. My legs were so swollen. We were glad we escaped the heat and stench of the train, but we did not know a more horrible fate awaited most of us.

We arrived in a little Austrian village called Mauthausen.

They marched us through the village, with the only sound coming from our feet hitting the gravel and the guards yelling at us to keep up the pace. This hamlet reminded me of books I had read as a child. It was like Hansel and Gretel, a beautiful storybook village, with neat gardens surrounding colorful houses with steeply pitched roofs. Although as we passed the homes and shops, the shutters were tightly closed and none of the villagers showed themselves, despite the noise, as we proceeded through the town invisible.

The air was so still. As we trudged along, I tried to rid my mind of any worries of what lay ahead. The countryside was beautiful with the mountains in the distance. Apple orchards lined our path, but we not dare pick them. Even though I was extremely hungry and thirsty, I managed to keep up with the others. Days ago, we had finished the food Schindler had given us for our journey.

We went up the hill and saw what looked like a castle, as if the sky was made out of stones that loomed in the dawn. Mauthausen was a camp made of stone walls, crowned with a high voltage barbed wire. This fortress looked invincible, frightening and foreboding. As the sun burst over the peak, we entered the camp through a drawbridge. Along the bridge, we saw SS. As we were walking, they kicked us all the way, like footballs. We did not know what was to be. Life without Oskar Schindler was about to begin. We would learn all too soon this deadly quarry would challenge our strength and courage.

There were two big buildings on the right-hand side. We did not know what they were. We soon found out one was the bathhouse and one was the crematorium, so we thought they are probably going to kill us here. Carrying submachine guns, they lined us up behind the buildings. We stood and waited there the entire day and it started to get dark, as evening came. In between the buildings, there was a 40-foot breezeway. We could see that someone was coming out.

One by one, an SS guard stood on a high platform with a giant, powerful light and inspected everyone's mouths, looking for diamonds or valuables that prisoners might attempt to conceal. It seemed as if the procedure took hours, and still, no water. They weren't talking to us, yet they weren't killing us. Some were walking out barefoot and in German flannel underwear.

This Polish person, who was a prisoner, a sweeper, he comes over and said, "If they don't kill you, that means the war is ending. That means no Jews are here." That was a mixed, horrible feeling.

While I waited to be inspected, still very thirsty, I noticed an older prisoner watching us from a window higher up in the camp kitchen. Perhaps against all good sense, I begged him for water, with my voice cracking from the thirst. Silently, he made a motion, touching his finger, as if to say, "Pay me and you will get your water." He knew the Germans were about to take anything of value we had and managed to bring with us. He saw the opportunity to get his hands on them first. He also knew he could be gravely punished if one of the patrols observed this forbidden exchange.

I had some Polish zloty smuggled in the lining of my coat, left over from the black market at Schindler's camp, which might have been completely worthless in Austria. There had been a thriving black market at Schindler's factory, which had allowed some of us to get money. I, like a number of others, bought tobacco from Polish workers and made cigarettes by hand.

I would later come to find out at Mauthausen, the black market currency was cigarettes. For half a cigarette, one could buy a bowl of soup or a spoon of salt or sugar. A piece of bread cost two or three cigarettes.

The prisoner looked at my crumpled bills with disdain, as no doubt he was hoping for gold or a diamond or two. He did not want to take it, and finally took the bills as I said, "Please, please, I am very thirsty," and handed him my soup dish. He filled my soup dish with water, placed it on the windowsill and disappeared. While the guards hadn't noticed this transaction, my fellow prisoners did. As I reached for the dish, everyone began scrambling and jostling like animals, with desperate hands scratching and clawing at me for a few soothing drops. As a result of the pandemonium, most of the water spilled to the ground and the little I was able to drink would have to last.

After the inspection was completed, we went to the bathhouse, they shaved us, and we took a bath. They shaved our bodies completely with a straight razor and our hair like the marines twice a week, every Wednesday and Sunday. There was a prisoner who lined us up to inspect us, and our hair, to see that everyone was shaven properly. Right in the center of our heads, they shaved a row, two inches wide, like Mohawk Indians in reverse. I felt so strange, sitting there, seeing my hair fall away, but I was too nervous to really care. The idea was that we looked very conspicuous and would not be able to escape unnoticed.

We were herded along to another room where we were handed flannel underwear. Although what I received was far too small as I was 6-feet tall, it was a welcomed relief to the filthy, lice-filled clothes I had glued to my body through countless days. The dirt and odor had been unbearable.

It seemed that this first day at Mauthausen would never end. As I stood in yet another line to register for my block, I wondered why the Germans were going through all of this trouble if they planned to kill us right away. Perhaps this is a good sign. Perhaps we would be able to live awhile longer.

I was not alone at Mauthausen. With me, standing in line, were my seven closest friends since the war had first thrown us together working at the Luftwaffe airport base outside Krakow. We made a pact to try and stand by each other to survive, where we would spend the last seven to eight months of the war. Standing nearest to me was Ben Friedman. Beyond him, was Otto Nussbaum, Philip Getzler, Isidor Neumark, Fred Landestorfer, Henry Rosenstein, all Polish Jews from Krakow, and a German Jew named Amper.

We all gave our names and occupations and registered as machinists, thinking this would make us the most useful and a means of keeping us together. After all, this strategy worked before when we were chosen for Schindler's factory. If we appear to be valuable, maybe our chances for survival would increase.

Our German jailers next marched us to the barracks, Blocks 21-25. These were low, stone buildings, with nearly flat roofs made of wood. My new home would be Block 22. At first, there were no bunk beds or anything. We wore pajamas and we had no shoes. We left our shoes in the bathhouse and were barefoot.

Barbed wire connected each building to the high stone wall, creating a separate yard for each barrack. To wander the yard of another block was strictly forbidden, punishable by whatever means the barrack's kapo decided upon. The kapos, prisoners themselves, held sway over life and death. They could make your existence unbearable or perhaps a bit lighter. The German guards might sit high in their towers overlooking the camp, but inside it was the kapos who could decide who shall live or die, with little interference from their German lords. Even though they had better clothes and got the best food, they were still prisoners and eventually would share our fate.

A kapo was a Nazi concentration camp prisoner who was given special privileges by the SS to supervise the other prisoners or forced laborers, limiting the need for SS personnel. Kapos were typically spared physical abuse and hard labor. The hierarchy was designed to turn kapos against fellow prisoners, as kapos were common criminals and were often brutal to fellow inmates. A lagerkapo was the head kapo. A lagerführer was the head SS officer assigned to a camp.

At Mauthausen, the Germans distinguished prisoners by colored triangles sewn on their uniforms. Red triangles marked political prisoners, yellow for Jews, purple for Jehovah's Witnesses and other clergymen, pink stood for homosexuals and green marked criminals. Letters inside the triangles identified the prisoner's nationality. They were prisoners of different nationalities and none of them were Jewish prisoners: German, Austrian, Spanish and Czech. You could call them criminals.

At the barracks, there was a private search by these trustees. The trustees – the most horrible people – gave the most horrible experience. This was the most degrading search of all. One by one, we sat on a little stool and there was a Spanish-speaking person who looked in everyone's rectum. Among all of us, they found a total of five diamonds. So far, I had managed to save pictures of my family; my last possessions from my home and all I had left of my brief childhood. I had smuggled and carefully wrapped these family photos in paper in my rectum, thinking they would be safe. They were looking for diamonds, but I had pictures, which were as precious as diamonds to me. I knew I had to dispose of the pictures or face a most certain beating, if not worse. My heart broke yet again as I slowly made my way to the toilet and flushed away the last part of my life that made any sense. This saved me from punishment, but only reopened the wounds and brought back the memory of watching my mother and sister being deported.

The first of many beatings at Mauthausen took place shortly after they had taken us to the showers. After showering, I returned to the room where we had left our clothes, looking for a belt I had left behind. Without warning, a Czech kapo prisoner began beating me with his fists. I said, "Why are you beating me? I am just looking for my belt." He said, "Let me tell you something: don't ever say 'mine' again at Mauthausen." This was because I had said, "my belt." He gave me a message, alright. "Don't ever say 'mine,' because nothing here is yours." I understood Czech, so I knew what he was saying.

I can never erase my memory of the first night in the barracks. The prisoners far exceeded the number of spaces in the bunks. They made us lie head-to-toe, like sardines, sleeping four to a bunk, three stories high, stacked like shelves. With my legs so badly swollen, I knew it would be impossible for me to sleep in those conditions. It was then I noticed a space under the bed of bunks, which was narrow, but big enough to accommodate my slender body. I squeezed in and went right to sleep, thinking I had discovered a suitable cubbyhole. Unfortunately, the men above me were jam-packed so tightly together in the bunks and they were too ill or too afraid to go to the bathroom in the night, so I awoke totally soaked in urine. Yet, the conditions were very clean there, even if it reeked of chlorine disinfectant.

And so ended my first day at Mauthausen, covered in human filth, not knowing the worst was yet to come.

The next night, I slept again on the floor, but this time among the horde of men, not under a bunk. Not only did I escape the nightly shower of filth, but I could more easily make my way to the toilets when the need arose. This was the case the second night, but as I waited my turn in line, another surprise which I could not prepare for, waited for me. The kapo of the barracks happened to be walking by, and without warning, he struck me on the chin with all of his force, knocking me to the ground. He was reputed to have been a heavyweight fighter in Vienna before the war. He simply walked away, without speaking, as if nothing happened. No matter how careful one was, there was little protection against the frequent and random acts of violence.

We were pushed around, kicked, beaten and tortured by the trustees or the kapos. It was horrible. Although unlike Plaszow, most of the prisoners at Mauthausen were not Jews. There were German Christians, Russians, Dutch, Czechs,

86

Italians and Poles, many being intellectuals or political prisoners. There was a small compound of British and American P.O.W.s, but their location was about a quarter of a mile away and we never got close enough to learn about them. We did see women occasionally, but they weren't prisoners, but girlfriends of the SS officers.

At Mauthausen, a Polish officer carrying a broom told us we were the first transport of Jewish people who were not killed. "We exterminated the Dutch and Belgian Jews over there, and you were the first group not to go to the crematorium."We speculated that perhaps he foreshadowed the end of the war. Then, some nice German prisoner gave us advice on how to behave at camp: "If someone tries to kill you and if you're at gun point, just run."

Supposedly, no one ever escaped Mauthausen. Well, except for the oft-told tale of the man who escaped in a sewer pipe on a truck. Hopefully, he did.

STONES

These are a few of my miracle stories, because one could call it miraculous how I survived this horrible place and these incredible situations. I was in Block 22 in Mauthausen. When we first arrived from Plaszow, we wore no clothing except for flannel underwear issued to us. We walked around barefoot waiting for an assignment. For the first few days, there was nothing to do but lie down idly in the sun waiting for the future, not knowing what was going to be or what they were going to do with us. Then began one of the worst chapters in my life as a prisoner of the Germans.

The guards were watching us between the two barracks and catching people to work. They began grabbing us at random. It was just like a Western movie. They were corralling us like a bunch of horses or cattle before we were branded. I cannot imagine why, for the first few days, not to be called. I was always somewhere, like one of those white horses or cows that managed not to get too close to the gate.

Friends of mine were called and given the uniforms and they went to the quarry to carry stones. When they came back after the work in the evening, they would tell stories of the impossible conditions. They said it was about the worst thing they have ever done. I mean, we could stand the shootings, being shot at, being pushed and being kicked, but this work was murderous. They all felt that they would not be able to make it and would probably perish in a few days. Either they would be shot or they would be pushed down the quarry.

Then one day, the captors grabbed me too and I could not escape from the group. They gave us smelly, old uniforms from Soviet prisoners of war. As they rushed us to put them on and get us ready to leave, we had little time to wonder what had become of the previous owners of these tattered, torn rags. Putting on a dirty uniform in itself was a horrible punishment and to wear something that many, many people had already worn before. It was never cleaned, never washed and full of lice. It was unbelievable to describe just the feeling to put something like that on your body. On the back of the uniforms was painted KG, or *Kommanditgesellschaft*, which in German meant limited partnership. We weren't numbered yet, so they gave us temporary numbers on a piece of chain. Still, we had no shoes.

We were a group of 400 people. I remember, exactly, 400 people. Each 100 were supervised by one kapo, one of which was carrying a stick. We were all waiting for the gate to open to go outside, and as soon as it did, they ordered us to run. Barefoot, we had to run more than a mile to the rim of the quarry. That did not mean we could flee from there because there were towers around us and there was no way of escaping. This was in the area of the canyon at Mauthausen. At the edge of the quarry, when we looked out, it looked like a small Grand Canyon and we were standing on the top. Of course, it didn't compare to the Grand Canyon, but it was an enormous area with clay and rocks and different little carts we called *waggons* in German, like a little bucket on a truck to load stones.

An SS guard in a khaki uniform ordered us to descend into a lower pit where prisoners broke bigger rocks with sledgehammers. To get down to the quarry of Mauthausen, we walked the infamous stairs, which were chiseled from the rock walls. One was two feet wide; one was probably a foot wide or less. There were 186 steps – the so-called "Stairs of Death" – which were incredibly difficult to maneuver. As soon as we went down the stairs, we all ran to a big hole to fetch the stones or rocks. Those who had been there before knew what to do. The goal of the SS was to make us carry these broken stones to an unnecessary destination, back up the same 186 steps, just to torture us. It was pure nonsense.

It was unnecessary to bring a stone to just dump it on a pile of stones somewhere else. They weren't using the quarry at the time for any building purpose or construction. Although the camp itself wasn't wired, it was built with walls from the quarry. They said that for every stone that was in the wall, there was one human being that perished at Mauthausen.

Looking down below, dead bodies were spread about and one was lying at the very bottom covered with pieces of paper from a sack of cement. No doubt, these victims were either pushed or slipped from the heights above. On this, my first trip to the quarry, I was frightened. I was terrified. I thought maybe I won't be able to make it to the end, and if I do, they will kill me on the way if I can't follow orders.

Meanwhile, several prisoners with sledgehammers were going about their business, breaking the rocks nearby. We got orders to carry one stone at a time. The experienced prisoners knew what to get. They would go down deep where the guys were with the sledgehammers and they would give them an appropriate size of rock to carry. Not knowing anything about it, I was so chicken, I didn't know what size to take. If you have a very heavy rock, you can't carry it up all those steps . . . or you have too small a rock, you are going to get beaten for it, or pushed or shoved down the quarry. It was very difficult to decide. It wasn't like you could put a stone on a scale and know exactly how much you could carry all the way back up.

The guards allowed us a short break while they went among the other prisoners, grouped in fours, inspecting rocks to be sure they were large enough. Finally, I grabbed a stone. I thought this one looked mediocre, like it was big enough and I could manage it. As I started walking to get in line, a guard stopped me with a whip in one hand and pistol in the other. He began berating me in German and beating me, saying that my rock was too small. My heart leaped into my throat and I dropped my stone and began searching for a more suitable one. All the while, the guard yelled at me and threatened to kill me if I did not work hard enough.

Prisoners carry large stones up the "stairs of death" (Todesstiege) from the Wiever Graben quarry at the Mauthausen concentration camp. *[1942, United States Holocaust Memorial Museum/Archive der KZ-Gedenkstaette Mauthausen, Washington, D.C.*

By this time, most of the prisoners had lined up waiting for their agonizing journey to the top of the quarry. I was the very last prisoner at the bottom of the pit, still searching, searching, and not knowing what rock to get. I had asked my friends, "Is this good enough? Is it big enough?" They told me, "No, it's not big enough." You know everybody had self-interest to find the right stone. Frantically, I kept looking for a rock small enough to carry safely, and at the same time, large enough to satisfy the screaming guard.

Gripped with panic, all of a sudden, something came to my mind. I went and got the same stone. I think the "man upstairs" told me to. Looking back, I don't believe it myself how I came up with this idea. The only way I was going to survive this would be to take the same stone again. I returned to the rock I originally chose and carried it differently than before. I ran past the guard and toward the back of the line. At any moment, I thought I would hear an order to halt shouted behind me, or I would feel the snap of the guard's whip against my back. Luckily, none of those horrible things happened.

I still had to get in line, so I went to my group and I tried to sit on my stone. Unfortunately, I didn't have enough time. The whistle blew and everybody got up to stand right behind their stone. An SS, the inspector general, in the khaki uniform went from the beginning of the line to the end, inspecting every rock. He then stopped and began beating a few people with a whip, just beating, beating, and beating. They each threw down their stones and began looking for larger ones.

I really began to panic. I was one of the last ones the SS inspected. I think there were maybe just a few prisoners behind me. One of my friends next to me said, "He's crazy, he'll kill you." I stood there and hoped that if I positioned my same stone at the just-right angle, it would look larger.

The SS may have recognized it, but he really couldn't see it. Perhaps the guard was distracted and didn't notice the sleight of hand I had played. He looked at me, looked at the stone, then just looked me right in the eyes and blew the whistle ordering us to go.

I carried that stone and made a first: we had to go up the steps — and I took the same stone — and it was unbelievable. Especially in the brutal heat of August (1944), it was excruciating to keep carrying, and carrying and carrying it. We were not allowed to set it down. You could not rest with it. It was about three or four miles with that stone.

My primary punishment that day was the raw and bleeding feet that all of us working in the quarry suffered from. I was thirsty, hot and it is impossible to explain how hard it was to walk barefoot among the little rocks and stones. Maybe a villager or farmer who was accustomed to go barefoot could manage, but for us it was impossible. My feet were bleeding, of course I couldn't walk fast, and my arms were aching in punishment. I kept walking and dragging and dragging, and finally we got to the destination. We dumped our stones on another pile of rocks and we turned around.

We all line up again, the whole 400 in the field near the quarry, and then they say *"Laufen!"* which means "run" in German. "Don't walk, you must run, run, run." So we did.

I made my second trip. Because I knew better, I was faster and I got down the quarry and grabbed a proper sized stone. I knew from experience what it was going to be. Three times more that day (and twice the next) I went down into the abyss, not knowing if I would return safely to the top. After two days, I knew I would not survive this work in the quarry. I wasn't as worn out as the poor people who made six trips a day. It was unbelievable. I was all sore from the beating. I was suffering. I can't even find an expression for it? I was disgusted and totally mentally and physically destroyed. Unless I could find a way to somehow avoid being sent back, the next day could be my very last.

I came back to the barracks and saw we all had to return the uniforms, but I decided to do something about it. Out of desperation, I devised a plan that I hoped would keep me from this certain death.

The next morning, before we were marched out to the quarry, I took off the Soviet uniform and dumped it through a bathroom window. At the next group in Block 23, they didn't know my name. They didn't know my number. The people who were in their underwear were the ones who had never been to the quarry, so I looked like I was with the people who never went. It was terrible what I did, but I wanted to save my life. So that is what I did. Dumped the uniform. It was a big risk. If someone had seen it, I would probably have been beaten. This was all inside the block and one of the kapos they say was a murderer, about 6'5" tall, and supposedly a Viennese prizefighter. He would probably kill me for that, but look, you take a chance.

I went outside the next morning and they are lining up the people in uniforms again to take them to the quarry. I am worried that they will recognize me when I wore that uniform. I believe there was about eight of them; they were all with the sticks and rubber whips. They are lining up the prisoners and making orders. "Chinatown, check." They needed x-amount of people, just like cattle.

I found a rag and a pail inside the bathroom on a rack. I took the pail and filled it up with water. I went outside the barrack and began washing the windows and walls, as if I had been assigned to perform this task. While they were catching people, lining them up, beating them, screaming and yelling about to take them to the quarry, I was by the wall washing windows. As they marched off and rounded the gray stone wall of the next barracks, I thought to myself, "I've been saved!" I kept my head down cleaning, going from one window to the next, slowly, methodically washing each pane. It was a big barrack, so by the third day, I was still washing windows. I managed to be temporarily spared and didn't carry stones for three days. Being conniving is an honest thing in a camp if you are trying to survive.

Finally, the man who was in charge of assigning prisoners to clean the interior and exterior of the barracks, a Russian Ukrainian kapo, spotted me. I couldn't speak or understand Russian then. That was my first experience with Russian people. Certainly, this is no reflection on the Russian people, because there are good people. But he was a bastard. A tall guy, typically, I should think built like a strong man. None of those people had any lack of food or drink and they were not skinny like all of us prisoners. They were all fat, fat enough. Very seldom were any of the trustees skinny, maybe by nature. They were all fat as if they had an ample amount of food to eat. Of course, they ate their food and they ate our food.

Since I couldn't speak Russian, I didn't know what he was saying. Basically, he said, "What are you doing here? Who told you to do that?" I answered, "One of the kapos." Since he was in charge of the interior and exterior of the barracks, he assigned prisoners to washing windows and therefore knew I was an imposter. Without warning, he punched me in the gut with such force I doubled over. He pulled me by my shirt, and he beat me with several more blows to my back, hit me in the face, kicked me in the chest, before he pushed me aside and swaggered away. "That will teach you not to loaf off around here," he said over his shoulder. Imagine a prisoner beating a prisoner: it hurts. We got in a good boxing match. You know, every time a prisoner beat me, it hurt twice as much as when I was beaten by the SS man. For the SS, it was part of his duty to beat, but this guy, a prisoner with intense rage. I was totally disgusted. He grabbed the pail from me and tells me, "Don't you ever do that. If I see you again, I'll kill you. I shoot by the windows." I was very lucky that I managed not to go with the stones for three days and get the beating. I was just thinking, how long can I evade going to the quarry?

The situation there was that you work all day long when you are assigned to the yard. You don't dare go to the barracks, except to go to the toilet, and one day they beat me for that, too. The barracks were only to go to sleep. By the wall at the end of the block of the barrack, people were lying down taking a break in the shade, but it was still very, very hot. It must have been the equivalent of 95 or almost 100 degrees. So I lie down there in the shade among 15 or 20 prisoners, most of whom were not feeling well or were sick. I decided to keep lying down and not to go away from there too much, because I didn't want to be seen, grabbed and beaten for why I wasn't in the work detail.

The kapos were looking to take more people to carry stones. They brought more old disgusting uniforms. They wanted to torture everybody. There was no way to escape. I continued to lie down among the sick and I was moaning, holding my stomach, pretending to be ill. I showed the guards a piece of bread I had saved from breakfast, telling them I was too sick to even eat. My plan worked. The kapos went from one to the next to pull people who were lying down and ignored me. They came to me and I acted and said, "Oh, oh, oh." I repeated the ruse and pretended to be sick for about five or six days, so I didn't have to go to the quarry. Believe it or not, I don't think there was anyone who went to the quarry as little as I did. For those who were sick, the guards never sent them to the hospital for treatment.

The Germans were continuously running short of healthy workers for the quarry. Since Mauthausen had several satellite camps to support, prisoners were constantly being transferred. Many of these sub-camps had been established to specifically meet the needs of German manufacturers who had contracted with the SS for prisoner labor. The prisoners usually found themselves working at war-related jobs, such as munitions factories.

One morning, when the kapos lined up the prisoners to work in the quarry, they realized not enough healthy prisoners remained to make up a full contingent. One of the kapos began passing among us sick, looking for people to add to the work party. I realized this was the head kapo from the barrack, the Viennese prizefighter I had so painfully encountered a few nights before. I tried to melt into the crowd, so he wouldn't notice me.

Now, he recognized me and said, "Du! Dich habe ich lange nicht gesehen!" which means "You! I haven't seen you for a long time!" He hit me, as I tried to run away. He caught me immediately, forced me down and put my head between his legs so I could not escape. The other trustees came and took turns beating and kicking me. It was unbelievable the beating I got. The blows were so hard and the pain was so intense, I soiled my trousers. And yet, the beating continued. I was completely demolished, mentally and physically.

I managed to turn loose, but I don't remember how. Humiliated and in pain, I limped back to the crowd and tried to merge in with the people ready to go to the quarry.

I was then grabbed by the last one of the trustees who was watching. He had a 1-inch square stick made of very hard wood and he practiced hitting people over the head and splitting open their foreheads. This was his specialty.

He was a prisoner in a pink shirt and held me up with one hand by my shirt, and was about to split my forehead open with his stick, perhaps killing me or leaving me with a scar for life. All of the sudden he whispered to me, *"verschwinden,"* which meant "disappear" and he let me go. Now the reason he did that, because he was a homosexual and apparently, he liked me. I was a young fellow and it was similar to a guy liking a pretty girl. Of course, I had never been involved and never would be in that and luckily, I was never forced into anything like that. Later he approached me and said, "You are so good looking," flirting with me, hoping I would give in to his advances. While I didn't succumb, a number of inmates did, accepting a reward of more lenient treatment for sexual favors. These prisoners received more food than the rest of us and the kapos permitted them to remain inside during the day, while the rest of us were only allowed in the men's room.

So, to the others, he was very vicious. He was a German prisoner among the other Czechs, Poles and Spanish who were homosexual prisoners the Nazis had consigned to the concentration camp system. We called them the "angels of murder." These were prisoners and murderers and they of course had it good, because they had special quarters, special food, wonderful clothes and they drank and fooled around with some of the young prisoners because they were homosexuals.

This group then ordered us to carry two stones. They sent me down to the quarry. The SS man at the quarry was the same guy, always the same guy. It was like he was a specialist in that. We made a few tours with two stones, not one. Which wasn't very easy. It was very difficult to adjust to two stones, with one in one hand and one in the other arm and very awkward. I dragged my bruised and beaten body up the quarry steps three times that day. Where the energy came from, I cannot explain. What became increasingly apparent was that I would not, could not, survive much longer working in the quarry.

Perhaps it was this realization and a growing desperation that caused my friend Ben Friedman and I to risk a certain death. It was a scorching hot day, as we hauled rocks in the searing sun and we were parched. It was so hot, it was unbelievable. We were beyond hunger, but so very thirsty. No water in sight. We filed like geese to head back to the barracks. Ben and I saw a wide-open window at one of the SS officers' barracks. They had very long windows in the barracks and we were thinking it would be nice to get a drink of water. Ben said, "Sam, you keep watch," and he said, "Where's the SS man?" I said, "Well, he's behind us, he's going to be here any minute." We both put our stones on the ground and each took turns hopping through the window to grab a drink of water. We got back out, unnoticed and continued marching in line with our stones. It was a tremendous risk, but we did it just for a drink of water.

As we were returning to the main camp, we stood in line at Mauthausen's big main gate. On the left, there was a swimming pool for the Germans, for the officers. Imagine to be able to go swimming! The very thought of it seemed so out of place – here, where normal human behavior was only a memory. We couldn't see the water and just the banister, but we knew there was a pool because ladies were walking around in bathing suits.

This beautiful young German woman leaned over the banister and looked at our half-starved bodies in disbelief. We pleaded with her and said, "Wir sind sehr durstig. Wir brauchen dringend wasser," which meant, "We're very thirsty, we need water desperately."

She didn't speak to us and disappeared, so we thought for sure we had frightened her away. Within a few minutes, much to our surprise, the fire brigade made up of camp inmates arrived and they sprayed us with water like they were spraying a building on fire. They kept moving back and forth, the force of water through our mouths. It was almost impossible to drink, yet we stood with our mouths wide open, hoping to catch every drop we could. Eventually, they brought kettles that were filled with water and all of us managed to get a drink individually. Apparently, she was quite offended, felt sorry for us and evidently had a lot of influence, but who knows who she was. It was a miracle she was there. She was a good human being. Amid a sea of horror, an occasional island of humanity remained.

The next morning, we lined up at the gate to go to work in the same situation of carrying around stones. Before I suffered what was sure to be an inevitable fatal fall from the deadly steps of the quarry, the Germans came with an unexpected announcement: "Juden tragen keine Steine mehr," which meant, the "Jews will no longer carry stones."

Instead, the Dachau will carry the stones. A new group of prisoners from the Dachau concentration camp had arrived. Dachau was the first Nazi concentration camp in Germany and the purpose here was to show the people the difficulties of Mauthausen. The Jews would now be used for other jobs and sent to satellite camps like Linz, Melk, Gusen, Gunskirchen, St. Georgen, Hartheim, Ebensee or San Valentin.

We could hardly believe it when we heard this news. Although we were told Jews would no longer be sent to the quarry, it was difficult to imagine that they may send us to do something even worse than carrying stones. We then waited to be assigned to a new job.

I knew I would never survive continuing to work in the quarry. Only after the war, I learned that the quarries at Mauthausen generated among the highest number of casualties of all the German concentration camps including Auschwitz, Treblinka, Bergen-Belsen and Belzec.

Yet, somehow, I survived.

MORE FROM MAUTHAUSEN
BLOCK 22

Shortly after taking us off the quarry duty, but before being transferred to another camp, I was sent to a secret destination and I remember it was much better work than carrying stones.

Outside the walls of the main prison at Mauthausen was a huge area which the Germans controlled for the forced labor camp, including a quarry and a vast forest where the prisoners were cutting a lumber supply for the Germans.

The guards came and picked us up. They walked 150 of us to a warehouse with a camera so we could not escape. The man in charge was sort of a mediocre kapo, a short little guy, and he lined us up. We counted off 150, and each third he appointed a chief, one prisoner to be in charge of that group. With me being tall, I got the assignment, unfortunately. He said, "Pick up a stick and you'll be in charge of the group, which means you'll be a kapo."

I definitely didn't want to be a kapo. It wasn't my choice. He was screaming at me because he assigned me and I had to pick up a stick. I couldn't brutalize fellow prisoners. I was only 19 years old, but I had suffered more physical and emotional pain in the last five years than anyone should endure in his or her entire lifetime. I just couldn't cause anyone to suffer. I wouldn't have hurt anybody, but I was kind of worried that I may have to and be forced to do some dirty work. Yet, I couldn't tell the guards I would not be a kapo, so I reached a compromise. I carried the stick in my left hand and went on to carry blankets over my shoulder like the others.

At the warehouse, each of us had to carry 20 blankets to an unknown destination. We walked out of the main gate of the camp and went several miles into the woods, sweltering like pack animals in the August heat. I walked with a stick and watched my group. We carried blankets for about three or four miles and dropped them at a giant tent, and made three or four trips back and forth carrying more blankets. It was almost impossible to carry 20 blankets together folded and they kept falling down constantly.

After a day of work and darkness began to fall, the SS guards came over to round us up. It was routine to then count out the prisoners. This was done constantly at camp and could take hours. Several times they counted us and each time the count was only 149. One is missing. They counted again and again, and each time, they grew more agitated and outraged. Obviously, a prisoner had escaped and no doubt the guards would blame us in charge of the detail. One kapo kept yelling, screaming, and liked to beat us up. I told him I remembered who my prisoners were and very slowly he said, "Keep your mouth shut." He went on to another group and another group, and we were still missing one prisoner. He was furious. He said, "How am I going to go back if I have a prisoner missing?" He was getting really vicious, this little guy. Even though I could account for the people assigned to me, I knew there could be deadly consequences from an escape under our watch.

As the guards kept yelling louder and louder, out of the blue, a tall, crisply dressed German officer emerged from the forest, followed by a few subordinates. Young, blond and very handsome, he walked into our storage house and some of the prisoners from Prussia recognized him immediately: SS Obersturmfuhrer Ekhard. He had been sent to the Plaszow labor camp to relieve the sadistic Amon Goeth, who stole everything from the diamonds confiscated from the prisoners to food supplies. Those who knew Ekhard said he had a reputation for being fair with the prisoners at the Plaszow camp.

He came over, looked at us among all the commotion, and simply said, "Oh, you're the guys, you're the prisoners from Krakow, so you must know me." It was as if he saw his relatives all of the sudden. He became very friendly, smiling and chatting with us and of course he asked, *"Was ist los?"* which means, what's cooking, what happened here. What is the problem? An SS man stepped out and he said that we are missing a prisoner. Ekhard turned his keen blue eyes first on the guards, then on the prisoners, to hear both sides of the story. I spoke up and suggested that perhaps the guards were mistaken about the original number in the group. The prisoners adamantly swore that no one had fled. We were right within the walls of the camp and wires, so there was no way anyone could have escaped. Nevertheless, it was a terrible thing because there were supposed to be 150 of us. The SS man he told me right away to keep my mouth shut and if that is accurate, that contradicted him. He said, "Well maybe he's right." The guy didn't like it of course, but he had no choice, as it was better to agree with me.

Without allowing the guards to take hasty punitive action, Ekhard led our entire party back to the main gate. As we arrived there, the SS went to the guardhouse window with "150" written on a little piece of paper. Looking at him, the man at the window had a note of 149. The guards consulted the log sheet. Of course, there was another SS behind that window and he said, "Oh sorry, we have made a mistake. It was 149." For once, the Germans' meticulous record-keeping habits worked in our favor. I am sure, had Ekhard not miraculously emerged from the trees when he did, the bloodthirsty SS guards would have administered their version of just punishment and I may not have survived to tell the story.

From this, I learned which one was the highest ranking, which I think was rank of a Colonel of the SS. I do not know exactly what rank Ekhard was, but from what I heard and read after the war, he was the one that came to Plaszow to make order. Among other things, he arrested Amon Goeth, who was one of the worst commanders of camps of anyone

I knew. That was the one and only time I saw Ekhard. Never again did I have to pick up a stick and be in charge of anything, thank God.

The next day (August 1944), all of the sudden, we took showers, shaved and we had to line up to be very clean. They brought bundles of uniforms. Each bundle consisted of a striped uniform, a pair of boots and a hat, just as you see in the movies. They kept calling us by name and threw our uniform to us like a football. Each uniform had a number and that was the year I got a uniform like everybody else. I put on my jacket, and being tall and I have long arms, it was a very short uniform, short pants and short jacket. My arms and hands were sticking out. There was no one who would exchange with me. A short guy wanted a large uniform because it would keep him warmer in the winter and he wouldn't exchange. I had to be satisfied with what I got. The pants were always about four inches too short. I looked like a circus clown. The jacket I could hardly button.

Then they gave me my number - 87064 - and that was my number to this day. It was just a piece of white cloth with a number and above it was painted yellow with a brush. This number became my identification throughout Mauthausen and a number I will never forget, with all of the atrocities to come. Our keepers never called us by name; they only used our numbers perhaps in an effort to dehumanize us and further justify our cruel treatment. I also have a tattoo from Schindler, which is a KL on my wrist meaning Konzentrationslager, the German word for concentration camp. Only the people who were in Plaszow got tattoos. Dr. Rubinstein had tattooed us at the order of the SS.

Now in our uniforms, we lined up, marched out of the gate, similar to when we first arrived there. They interviewed us and they wrote down our occupation the first day, but we didn't have numbers. Now, I was considered a prisoner with a number. In a previous statement, I said I was a machinist.

I was hoping they would send me to a place where I can work in a factory.

Samuel Soldinger's identification number at Mauthausen. The badges were sewn on uniforms with triangles: Sam's had "P" for Polish with a yellow stripe denoting Jewish.

They called my name, with a group of people, not all people from Block 22, but quite a lot of them. We walked down the hill out of the main gate on a beautiful day, all clean, beautifully dressed. Beautifully dressed, by comparison, as it was a paradise to be clean and wear a pair of shoes, which we hadn't worn for weeks.

At least we knew we were going somewhere, probably to work. They weren't going to put us in the ovens, so I knew that we survived that far. It was kind of a marvelous feeling. Walking down from Mauthausen, they had some apple trees on the way. We managed to gather a couple of apples and eat which was a wonderful thing to have an apple. A tiny little apple, a brand new apple, young apples.

They walked us to the railroad station and would you believe they put us in the passenger cars, sitting like passengers, regular people, not like cattle. Maybe a hundred of us at a time or more. Even with guards, we sat like passengers traveling about 30 miles to an unknown destination, just like going on an excursion, and of course, we had apples. The scenery along the way was beautiful, marking the contrast to our enslavement.

So the mood wasn't very bad. It felt somewhat promising. Who would have thought that perhaps there is some way we will make it through the war?

WELCOME TO LINZ

When we got to a camp called Linz III in September 1944, we were very lucky. It was a sub-camp of Mauthausen. I listed as a machinist and was assigned to work in a factory working on machinery and making windows for tanks. Thank goodness, this was about the last eight months of the war. The camp was built on the site of Hermann Göring Werkes, where they were making tanks and munitions. That was the purpose of the camp.

The day before we arrived, the Americans bombed the factory, so our first task became shoveling potholes and repairing the damage. The factories at Linz III were huge, red brick buildings. They were bombed occasionally, but the bombers seemed to avoid the barracks. When the Americans bombed the SS building in the spring, the SS made us sleep outside while they stayed in our barracks. They got their just desserts from the lice in our bedding.

It was a horrible, dirty camp. No food, no soap, no water, but we did get a bath once a month. Everything was muddy and we had one little wooden platform to walk on from barrack to barrack. There were only men, no women. There was one laundry for everyone, but no change of clothing whatsoever. It was hard to think of anything worse than the constant hunger, the dirt, and the lice. When it was a nice warm day, we would take off our clothes and underwear. The barracks were cold in the winter and we did not have any heat. In fact, the guard one time took out our barrack windows and locked them up in his office as punishment, so we slept without windows. As the winter temperatures plunged well below freezing, we smuggled in some wood and made a fire. It was unbelievable the torture and the persecution we suffered from the trustees, just as much as the Germans. Sometimes the trustees were even more awful than their SS counterparts were. One beat me once because he didn't like the way the door closed when I went to the restroom, so he hit me with a rifle butt. One of the SS officers in charge of our section of the factory was not only disliked by the prisoners, but his own men as well. His name was Winkler and one of the SS men gave us a matchbox to pick the lice off us and put in the box, then they emptied it in the officer's laundry. Soon, we saw him itching like the rest of us. Yet, one other SS guard, asked us to wire a reading light for him and he was most grateful, rewarding us with cookies.

However, the Germans, the Nazis, they use to walk around when there was an execution and it would be a whole parade. They caught one guy and made him walk around in front of the group to say "he is back" with a band playing behind him. Then they killed him. The band always played when there were hangings. On one German kapo shoemaker, they found a piece of leather cut from a broken belt in the factory in his pocket - enough to fix a pair of shoes - and they called for execution. Everyone had to get out of bed for the execution and he was hanged publicly before 6,000 prisoners. The Germans left his body hanging for several days in an area where we all passed regularly. It was unbelievable. And, there was always music.

We expected the Germans would kill all of the prisoners before the end of the war. Escape was possible, but the consequences discouraged us. I could have escaped going to the air raid bunker one night. A low-flying Russian plane attacked us with bombs and rapid gunfire. We all scattered and I was alone. I could have run away from the camp at that moment, but the Germans would have found and killed me. Instead, I walked back to the camp and the guards let me in without a problem when I explained what happened.

It was Christmas 1944 and they gave us a present, which was a log of lard, like a piece of bacon, which was the size of an aspirin box. Everyone just swallowed and devoured it, and unfortunately, everyone became indescribably ill with dysentery, including me. It was too much fat for our stomachs to handle. I lined up at the hospital. The main purpose was not only to get medication, but also to get a pass not to work the next day. There was no medication, so they gave us what seemed like some type of plaster of paris. They could not handle us all and said, "We can't take care of you now. Go back to your barrack. If we find out you're lying, you'll get 25 lashes, or you may turn to ashes." Well, of course, I was very sick. It was horrible. So I lined up again in the morning. They gave us the military lashes, and then put straw on the floor for us to lie down in an empty barrack. They brought us hot porridge and gave us good portions three times a day. That was a good fortune that they gave us good food. It was not a lot, but it was adequate.

Once I felt better, they needed people to help clean the hospital, so I volunteered. I was surprised they took me, because that was too good of a job for a Jew. I told this very nice Polish man, Sigmund, "Maybe you won't take me, because I am a Jew." It must have hurt his feelings. He said, "If you do good work, you can stay. If you're no good, I will kick you out."

I began as an orderly and cleaned day and night scrubbing floors, carrying portable toilets and warming cement blocks to place at the feet of sick prisoners. They put up bunks so everyone had a bed to sleep in. This is where I met another savior, a German Catholic priest by the name of Frank Kaufman. We met at the latrine and he guessed I was a Jew, "because of your nose." I thought he was anti-Semitic, but he turned out to be an angel like Schindler. Although he wasn't like Schindler, in that he was a political prisoner and yet very friendly. They said he was a bishop, a high priest, an older man. He was very dedicated to his job and helping people. He noticed the way I was cleaning and asked my name. I said, "Samuel." He didn't like it and it sounded too

Jewish for him apparently. He said, "It's not very good here. I'll call you Franz." He changed my name immediately on the spot to Franz and I was Franz from then on. Even after the war, some people called me Franz. He was a wonderful individual. He treated me like his own son and one time he even gave me the shoes from someone who had died, knowing I had none.

That's the way it was. I kept working and stayed at the hospital for about two months. It was hard work, but it was great compared to where I had been. The good thing about working there is that I was the one giving out bread and soup. If we didn't have extra bread, but we did have a little extra soup, I would add that instead. I honestly tried to help all survive, especially with the dysentery situation happening, so I did all I could. In my time there, I had to carry corpses to the morgue by myself. I don't know if I could do something like that today. I am here, still standing. I cannot believe I was in a situation like that.

Soon enough, a few weeks later, I had to leave the hospital. Kaufman said, "Franz, sorry that you have to go, but we can't keep you any longer. You have been a very good worker, but you have to go back to the factory. I still want you to come after hours when you are through at the factory. You can help us here, because we need your work very badly. There will be a bowl of soup waiting for you."

It was unbelievable. Just like that, I had two bowls of soup until the end of the war. Can you imagine? Two portions of soup? It wasn't that much soup, but it was like having not one Cadillac, but two. It was a very big thing. I don't think anyone today would eat soup like that, but it was something. It was water. Maybe you could find a little potato or maybe a little drop of meat. We lived on about 300 calories a day. I kept a little rock in my pocket to suck on when I got hungry. Some prisoners were so hungry that they ate dirt, cooked grass, rotten potatoes or just about anything. I never did that, which probably saved me. Skinny, I was probably half the size I am now. There was not one fat person, that was for certain.

By the middle of 1944, three external camps of the Mauthausen concentration camp had been erected in the city of Linz, Austria.

The first camp, in which up to 1,000 male prisoners were held, was constructed at the end of 1942 in order to utilize the slag from the blast furnace from the, Reichswerke Hermann Göring. The profits from the utilization of the slag was shared by Reichwerkes and the SS.

In the spring of 1944, at the behest of Hitler himself, the SS provided prisoners as laborers to extend the air raid shelters at the Märzenkeller. The approximately 380 male prisoners of this camp, which was named Linz II and was run by the SS, were housed right in the shelters themselves.

Not long after the Reichwerkes succeeded in getting further concentration camp prisoners as workers for the extension of the shed and for tank production at the subsidiary firm, Eisenwerke Donau (Danube Iron Works). By the fall of 1944, the specially erected camp Linz III housed more than 5,600 male prisoners.

In total, 800 prisoners lost their lives in the three camps.

A FEW LOOSE WIRES AND A LITTLE LUCK

I don't recollect how long it was, but the geography that I know now, it could have maybe been like 20 or 30 miles by train. We landed on the tracks right off of the camp on a street called, Linz Street, which was lucky, in the small town of *Klein Munchen*, which means, "little Munich." The area was full of giant industrial buildings they called Hermann Göring Werkes. There were giant factories and giant buildings that were isolated from civilization. We had to cross a small, tiny little, river; it could be a stream, but maybe a tiny river. It was about 30 to 40 feet wide.

Reichswerke Hermann Göring was an industrial conglomerate of Nazi Germany.

There was a long bridge and a camp surrounded by towers and wires. We walked into the Linz III camp and they lined us up like normal prisoners, counting us. They called it *count platz* which means a place where they take the inventory. Prisoners were counted twice a day. We were sitting there and they called my name. I was assigned to Block #2. Being with my friend Ben Friedman, we tried to be always together. He was also assigned to Block #2, except that being under "S" I was in a different block building. It was just across the yard from me. So we went over to our block. The man who was in charge was a German prisoner. He had a green triangle on which indicated that he was a criminal. He was very friendly, very nice and he welcomed us to join him at a large table. We sat there and he talked to us as if we were his relatives. Later, we found out what kind of a S.O.B. he was.

112

While we were there waiting for an assignment (we didn't know where we were going or what it would be), they came with the bookkeepers and they again wrote all kinds of information. We didn't fill out an application, but they were interviewing us again and asking us about our capabilities. Over the next couple of weeks, we just lingered there at that barrack, #2.

As we were sitting there at the table, day by day, this guy came in, a German. He claimed he was just recently arrested and he was the Chief of Vienna Police, which of course we couldn't prove. It was a strange and different feeling to be mixed with prisoners who were not Jewish. There was a handful of Jews among other religions and nationalities.

The food was the same and very little, very little soup. Fortunately, we were so clean, with new outfits, and we had a name. As new prisoners, they called us "Neuzugang - Neuzugang," meaning newcomers. Yet, we were still wondering what was going to be and the next day, we still didn't have a proper assignment.

They took quite a few of us with shovels and picks to do some repair work on the ground because just a few days before through an air raid, the lot was destroyed, the buildings were partially destroyed, demolished, and they had big holes in the walls. That is where the guards were staying, approximately 500 to 1,000 yards from the main entrance to the camp, which used to be some kind of a warehouse before the war.

We were working and suddenly an SS comes over with one of the prisoners (this guy had a red triangle which was political prisoner) we didn't have too many political prisoners, mostly criminals. The SS asked, "Are there any electricians among you? Ben had pursued an apprenticeship in the airport in Krakow where he worked in a shop. He knew a lot about electricity. I knew some basic electricity by digging cables, but very little. Ben tells me, "Sam, come on let's volunteer.

Why work here with shovels. Let's be electricians? Come on." I said, "Ben, listen, you're good, but I will be in trouble sooner or later." "Come on Sam, come with me." You know Ben was a very optimistic person. Always a wonderful friend and if I was with Ben, there was not a problem. There must have been some very good electricians among those people.

They chose six of us and they made three teams of two. Ben and I were a team. We followed the political prisoner who was the head of the electrician shop. He was a pretty gentle guy - I can't say that he was vicious - I know that after the war we embraced. Although, once he beat me up because he got aggravated. I didn't know what he wanted me to do. He didn't beat me up seriously, just slugged me once or tried to slug me. I do not remember his name, but basically, I gave him a star for being a decent guy. I can imagine, when you're in charge and you have somebody like me that can't really help, it was aggravating. Nevertheless, he didn't torture me. He did nothing. He just pushcd me in that sense, or screamed at me.

He gave us letters and each one of us was given a belt with parts and supplies. He ordered us to go up several floors in giant lifts, because it was a warehouse and the SS were sleeping on the floor in sacks, as there were no beds. He directed us on what to fix, what to repair. I was terrified I would get a big, serious assignment and I would not be able to do it. Luckily, I was the guy who carried the ladder for Ben and it wasn't bad, it was actually a good job.

One day we got a kick. Somebody called us names and tried to push us. One guy tried to push us down the steps as punishment, and then on the other hand, there was a guy who gave us a piece of bread. One guy gave us some cookies and gave us some apples. It was just unbelievable how those people were. There was one S.O.B. who was an impossible

114

hater - especially when he saw me - because they were not accustomed to having any Jews in that camp. There were 6,000 prisoners already in Linz III. One advantage I had with Ben is that we spoke some German. Sometimes when nobody was around, we would inquire and ask questions.

We were helping and making the most of our time there. There were shorts in the wires and the fuses and we fixed those for a few days. Then they called us and told Ben and I to go in a truck and drop off a marble plate inside the camp. It was the first building and was being converted to a guardhouse. We carried it in and left it there. We did not install it.

A few days later, a strange thing happened in the middle of the night. They woke me up in my bunk and all I hear is, "You, electrician, get up." All I see is this German kapo, and a student kapo and he was holding my belt with the tools. They say, "Get up, get up, hurry, hurry," *aufstehen sich beeilen.*" Keep in mind, Ben is on the other side of the barracks, because he was F (Friedman) and I was S (Soldinger).

Undoubtedly, I didn't have a choice. They allowed me to put my jacket on. I put on my shoes, but I wasn't allowed to tie them. I went with the shoelaces hanging, in my underwear and just a jacket. I am sure I wore a hat, because I could not be caught dead without a hat. I began to wake up, as they marched me in the cool dead of night to the guardhouse, the place where we dropped that marble piece a few days earlier. It's a large room surrounded by bunk beds, and of course, as they were marching me, there was absolutely no light in the camp. They had flashlights and whistles, and were running, like you see in the movies today.

I was thinking there was apparently some emergency, and I was about to tell them that two is better than one and we should get Ben. Then I thought, "How can I go and tell them that Ben is there, when I have volunteered as an electrician and I don't know how to fix it?"

Once we got to the guardhouse, I went with the guards, the SS officers, who were holding flashlights and pointing to the electrical board that I needed to fix. There was a little table that was mounted on another table, and they were very shaky. I began to realize a guard had been sitting on the table and must have shaken it, making the fuses loose. These were giant fuses. In inches, maybe 6" or 7" in diameter. There were white fuses, porcelain fuses for the main buildings and all kinds of lights indicating the wires and the different departments of where the power was going.

I had no idea how to fix the problem so I thought, "I know, I'll just pretend." What else can I do at this point? As soon as I noticed that table, I got a little encouraged as I saw the screws were loose. I took one at a time. I had a brush, I cleaned it up and I put new wire I had on my tool belt. There was nothing wrong with the fuses. There was a fresh wire, but nevertheless I put on a little heavier wire. I did the other one. I replaced the wire and as soon as I turned the other one on, the lights, everything, lit up. The whole room and the whole camp. Now, I would not be a very good prisoner to help my fellow prisoners who wanted to escape in a situation like that, but of course, I had no choice. I also did not believe that somebody was escaping. To the guards yes, but to me there was probably just something loose, which it was, a few loose screws.

Much to my surprise, they jumped at me, patting me, I heard one of them say, "Haben sie je so etwas wie das gesehen? Der Jude hat das gemacht." That means, "Have you ever seen something like that? The Jew did that." I mean because they were accustomed to believing that the Jews were not capable of anything.

With the electricity back on, I went back to my barrack and went to sleep. When I woke up the next morning, I tell Ben and my friends what happened. Oh, Ben was hysterical! He said I had a bad dream! I told them no, it really happened.

They just laughed and teased me! I knew the truth and that it really happened. Luck was on my side again.

This saved my life because some of the guards, I didn't know them, but now they remembered me. They were funny people, even the SS. One will kick you. One will kill you. One will respect you. We had 600 guards, which was one for every 10 prisoners. Every so often, a guard would talk to me because they remembered me, even though I had the mark of a Jew. Some of them were just like people. They would say, "Hi, you're the electrician, how are you?" Otherwise, they were miserable S.O.B.s, but some were human. You know, I just feel like it was my duty to tell the truth because they were like the beauty and the beast. I went to work the next day, fixing some new wires by the river. Ben and I were putting in new insulators and we came to the barracks for lunch. We lined up and got a bowl of soup like everybody else. We sat like hungry dogs, hoping that there would be a miracle and maybe we would get seconds. Second helpings were very seldom given to prisoners. If there were any leftovers, the person who was in charge had enormous power to do whatever he could with them. He would probably sell them for something to somebody who had cigarettes or money.

I sat there with all the prisoners, and everybody was happy, eating the soup. There was the kapo who was in charge of the Block, and his assistant Mr. Schrieber. They were the power of the Block. They were in charge of Block #2. After everybody got to eat, he normally called the people that work to clean up. Would you believe it, the first thing he called, he said, "The electrician from last night, come here." The electrician from last night, that's me! Here I go. I walk in and I get more soup and the people are staring at me - and that was how they knew it wasn't a dream. I will never forget it.

With all of the misery, we had a little bit of excitement and this was one of my exciting moments. Fortunately, it turned out to be something strange and funny. After a while, the Block kapo was very friendly. If I needed a pencil or a pen to borrow, I would go to him. He was a horrible man, but I was now a VIP to him. He was a different person already.

We continued working over there on the facility and I was with the electricians. All of the sudden, they called me and a few others to a different block with a horrible killer. They transferred eight of us to Block #6, and Ben was transferred to Block #10, because he was the other electrician. You see, different people went to different factories and different departments within Hermann Göring. I was transferred to a place called the BW, but they called it the BV1 department which was a giant kind of ground floor under the factories, a shop with hundreds of old and new machines, lathes, drills, you name it. The basic purpose of this factory was to make windows and other parts for tanks, because Hermann Göring was a tank factory.

They assigned me to a lathe and that was my job. I was fortunate, because my rheumatic fever was not giving me any trouble. I didn't have a fever and I worked very hard, even while the camp was filthy.

The conditions were unbelievable.

BOOTS

It was November 19, 1944, and I was in Block 6 at Linz III Camp. After more than four years of hard labor, I was hoping that this was the last winter at Linz III, which was a sub-camp of Mauthausen. Perhaps a miracle will come and we will get liberated from the murderers. We were always hungry. I would think to myself and worry about the winters. The snow. The sleet. How to keep warm. How to keep dry. And how to have a good pair of boots.

This story is one of my favorite experiences of how one gets a pair of boots, the impossible way. Just due to circumstances, I had no boots. Well, I had boots, but I did not have proper boots to survive much longer in terrible conditions. They were torn, tattered and patched, made from the scraps of people's belongings after the Nazis exterminated them. My boots were a kaleidoscope of different colors, made from pieces of the dead ladies' handbags stitched together. The SS took whatever scraps they could find and attached them to wooden bottoms and made shoes out of them. They were very uncomfortable, but I was grateful to at least have something. The seams opened up and the rain poured inside. Perhaps they would be good for two or three more weeks, but definitely would not last in a cold winter and the snows of Austria.

We had no socks, just a flimsy piece of paper stuck in our so-called boots. I bought a pair of socks later with some cigarettes I managed to get. (I bought the socks from an Italian guy who use to make pig salt. It was interesting to learn what people did before the war.) Of course, then the guards tried to steal my socks off my feet in the middle of the night, but they did not succeed.

Finally, a carload of boots came to the camp for all the prisoners. I was very happy about it. I just couldn't wait to get a new pair of boots. We all had smiles on our faces. We said, "We'll get boots! We'll get boots! We'll be able to go to work and not to feel the discomfort of the vicious cold."

A few days later, the boots appeared on many prisoners, consequently with smiles as if to say, "I have a new pair of boots." Some people were very happy because they had them. Our block only received a handful of them. Perhaps five or six people out of 600. Was there anyone to ask, "Give me a pair of boots?" Was there anyone to complain to? We just had to be quiet and wait for someone to call us to the block office.

That was the protocol of the elders on the block and ours was named Romi. He was a vicious killer, was confined for many, many years as a criminal and prisoner before the war, and was stationed here with many notorious criminals.

From what we had heard, and it was obvious, the share that Romi got for the 600 prisoners he somehow sold outside on the black market, probably to some guards or soldiers.

Therefore, there was no hope to get any boots. They were actually out of them. We were all very upset. It was very unfortunate being on what was considered the worst block of Linz III, Block 6, with a notorious killer. I just couldn't imagine how we would be able to survive the cruel winter. Of course, there were other problems of similar nature.

Days went by. Weeks went by. There were no other shoes to be received. The quota for Block 6 was given out. There was absolutely no way of getting shoes elsewhere. No place to shop. No place to get them for free. Perhaps my boots would last another year, or perhaps only another winter, or only one more day. Maybe by some miracle, somehow, somewhere there may be a chance I would get a new pair.

One Sunday afternoon early in December, the word spread that the lagerkapo, which was the head kapo of the concentration camp and the head prisoner, had some extra shoes to give away. I rushed to his office hoping that he was a nice man, who was by comparison, not a bad person. I do not remember his name, but he was not the kind of a man that would allow an injustice at that point and would give the shoes if he had them.

I went to his office and knocked on the door. I heard a voice . . . which meant, "Come in." I opened the door and to my bewilderment, the lagerkapo was lying in bed surrounded by visitors. The head lagerkapo, his two assistants and one other high-ranking SS officer, assistant lagerkapo and the lagerkapo's valet, all sitting and chatting. I was scared to death. I didn't know what to think. I panicked.

I spoke German, but not very well. I said, "Excuse me, I'm sorry, I didn't mean to bother you. I didn't realize that you were ill, forgive me, I'll come again."

"What do you mean, you'll come again?" the head SS Lagerführer said, "Come in, come in, talk to us. What is the matter? Tell us what happened."

"Well, I'm sorry, I'll come again. It's very unimportant, I didn't mean to disturb, please. It is completely unimportant. I didn't realize that you were sick. It's not an important matter to bother you. I'll come again when you get well."

I was in the lion's cage and had to get out of there.

The Lagerfürher said, "Well, tell us now. *Was ist los?* Tell us now."

"Well, I come here, I heard that the lagerkapo is giving out some boots. As you see my boots, I have not received them, and these are torn. I will have a hard time surviving and working. I heard that there were some extra boots to be given and that is what I am here for, but sorry again to bother you while you are sick. I didn't realize it, I'll come again."

He said, "Yes, it's true you have torn boots, terrible. Why didn't you get any boots?"

I said, "Well, some people got them, I just didn't. I can't tell you why. I don't know why."

Then he said, "Where are you? From which block are you?" I said, "From Block #6." All of them shook their heads. They all said the same thing simultaneously. "Ach, Romi, Romi again." The Lager Commander, the SS Commander, I don't recall his name. I believe he was executed after the war. At one point, he was a very bad man, but perhaps, feeling that the war was coming to the end, he was changing his attitude. I cannot describe it how nice and considerate he became. Then he grinned and said, "You go to Romi and you tell him that I Schutzlagerfürher order him immediately to give you a pair of shoes. Be sure to tell him immediately. If he doesn't, come right back here and tell us."

"Thank you very much. Thank you very much," I said. I walked out of the room. I can't describe whether I was a little scared or what was my feeling exactly. It was a terrible feeling. I was put on the spot. Should I go and tell Romi and be murdered, or should I just forget about it?

I spoke to some of my friends on the way. They said, "You're crazy, he'll kill you. Don't you dare go to him. Don't. Forget it. One way or the other, perhaps you will survive the winter. If you go and tell him that you talked to the commander — forgive me, to the Lagerfürher — if he won't murder you now, he'll murder you in a few days. He will find a way. He will find an excuse to murder you. Just let it go."

I took their advice and it was my own personal opinion not to go and tell him. I just forgot it and suffered and suffered. A few weeks later on Sunday afternoon, it was a day of shoeshine in the prison, and the shoeshine valet of the lagerkapo, a Polish man saw me, recognized me and asked, "What's the matter, you're still wearing the same old torn shoes. Why didn't you get any boots? What happened? How come you didn't come and say that you didn't get any? What is the matter with you?"

"What's the matter with me? Well, I am not crazy. If I go tell him, he will kill me. If he doesn't kill me now, he will kill me a few days later or a few weeks later. He won't forget. He will never forget and he will pay me back for it. I think I am better off taking my chances surviving the winter with the holes that I have and hoping for the best. I'm not going to go and take any chances."

The shoeshine valet said, "Well, come with me. Don't worry, come with me." I said, "Look, please, please, I'm not going to go with you. Please don't take me. Please, you know he'll kill me." I started to cry. I said, "Please." He said, "Nothing will happen to you. I take full responsibility. He will not touch you; he wouldn't dare. Please come with me." He begged me to come with him. He was a fine man. Older man. He insisted I go. I felt like running away from the situation, but I went along hoping perhaps it wouldn't be as bad. Maybe there was a chance.

It was just around the corner. He took me inside. Being a Sunday, Romi was taking a nap. He was always drunk. When he wakes, he was excited to see this prominent man, a valet of a lagerkapo, which was a very prominent man. A well-dressed man. "Oh, how are you? How have you been? It's nice to see you. Real nice to see you. What's the problem? Why did you come along with him?" The valet took him off to the side, whispered in Romi's ear and Romi smiled and replied, "Don't worry, we will. We'll take care of him. We'll give him the shoes, don't worry about it. Yes, we will. Give my best to the lagerkapo and don't be a stranger, come again."

When he left, Romi told all his assistants, his barber, his valet, his people that worked with him, pointed me out and he said, "Can you imagine this lousy Jew went and complained to the Schutzlagerführer (the camp commander). No one else but the Schutzlagerführer. Can you imagine that I didn't give him any shoes? He went and complained about me. How do you like that? Can you imagine?"

Romi, waving in his hand, had a one-inch electrical cable and pounded me with it several times. He kicked me. He pushed me. I was bleeding all over. He knocked me to the floor and started yelling and screaming. He ordered one of his assistants to make an appell, which meant, a roll call to gather all the prisoners from Block 6. The assistant blew a whistle and everybody lined up in between the barracks, about 600 men. I was on the other side of them actually. I could not stand on my legs. I just wished I were dead. I knew this was it. He will murder me right in front of them. I have never seen him this mad.

As he continued to yell and scream, he shouted, "Is there anyone here in the crowd who has something to complain about me, who didn't get any boots? Anyone who did not get any boots? Step up, you cowards." Just a handful got the boots, while the majority of people had boots like mine in very bad condition. Some prisoners even had their feet wrapped around with rags, but no one would dare to step out.

There were a few smug smiles among his assistants, which was normally the case. They wanted to show kapo Romi a sign of telling him he was right. Romi continued, "This lousy Jew went to the Schutzlagerfürher and he complained that I, Romi, the kapo of this block had not given him or anybody any shoes. How do you like that? He dared to complain that he didn't get any shoes. Do you know what he did to me? He spoiled my reputation. I have a reputation of being the best, the nicest, and he went and complained about me. He is going to pay for this."

He stepped over to me, hit and kicked me several times, and pushed me back to the ground. He blew the whistle for everybody to discharge, while I was left lying there bleeding, wishing to be dead. Now the other prisoners were afraid to come near me, or else would pay the consequences of being friendly. I just kept lying there, wondering what was going to be. I was swollen all over and in a lot of pain. It is impossible to explain what situation I was in. I just feared and wondered what was next. I figured he would leave me there until it got dark and perhaps then, he'll finish me, which he normally did to others.

All of the sudden, I see him coming out of the barrack with a big basket and he said to me, "You Jew, get up, get up, take the basket." I didn't know what he meant. I managed to pull myself together limping and staggering. I grabbed the basket. He said, "Follow me." *kommen mit.* I had to go by him. I still didn't know what he was up to or what would become of me. I kept walking the best I could muster. He was far ahead. I couldn't catch up with him, being dirty, muddy and bleeding.

And this was how I got a pair of boots.

The compound head, the Schutzlagerführer, performed the function of deputy to the commandant responsible for recommending punishments and was present at executions and when punishments were inflicted.

MY FRIEND HYME AND THE FRENCHMEN

In 1945, I am in Linz III, which was a sub-camp of Mauthausen, and it was in the spring, perhaps three or four months before the war ended. I had a friend and his name was Hyme Friedman. I know it was good to have a friend, to be with someone, talk to someone and not to be alone. Of course, there were other people who were friendly, but we were very close. We shared things. If I had some food, I shared with him, and when he had some food, he shared with me.

We were not friends before, although I knew him even before the war. He lived on the same street a few blocks away in Krakow. Being in the ghetto, on the same block, sometimes we slept next to each other's beds. He was a good companion and it was nice to be with him.

At Mauthausen, we talked a lot about politics and situations, hoping that the war would be over soon. We shared a lot of news from different people, and some Frenchmen told us that in fact, the city of Krakow was liberated and the war was coming closer to the end. There, hunger and thirst were perhaps the worst that we had experienced. Not enough food. We were just hoping that we would survive the rest of the war and possibly be liberated.

All of the sudden, Hyme became very friendly with a neighbor of ours, a guy by the name of Sigoulen who was from Zakopane (town in Poland). He was an older person by comparison; we were teenagers. One day I see Hyme sitting on a bed with a giant bowl of soup and both of them eating from the same bowl. I was stunned. I see them eating soup together, and I wanted to say, "Where am I?" I mean, what's the matter that I wasn't invited or told about it or something?

126

I felt very rejected in a terrible situation. I just could not barge in and I didn't want to make an issue about it. I didn't make any action, and if he's that kind of a guy, I simply realized that there was something going on. He became friendly with the other guy probably because the other guy had what we call, organization. That means he managed to get some soup somewhere whether for money or for something else, I have no idea. But they became very friendly. I was completely cut off from the friendship and was very isolated and was very unhappy. Then I would go to work by myself and it was just really upsetting me. It was a very, very bad psychological situation at a time like that to be double-crossed over some soup.

One day, I was near the kitchen and I see this guy signaling behind the back of the kitchen talking to two kitchen workers. Namely, they were both Frenchmen. They had the mark F — they wore black barrettes. Their clothing was a little better because they probably could afford it working in the kitchen and it seemed like one was very young. One was an older guy and one was young and it looked like a father and son combination. I could speak a little French, but didn't know French hand signals. Nonetheless, I saw them a few times working from the other kitchen bringing soup and my friend Hyme had a very nice dinner, while I starved.

When the war was over, I was in Italy for a while then went to Belgium on March 1, 1946. A few days later, I was walking down an empty street, then saw two people walking down this same street. I looked at them. I walked behind and listened to them for a while, because they did not know me. I knew them. They were the two Frenchmen. They were speaking Yiddish to each other, not French. Well, I could handle that better than French at the time, although I learned some French later. I stopped them and I said, "You probably don't know me, but I know you, you were at Linz III. You were working in the kitchen." "Yes!" They were all excited

and were very nice, wonderful people. They never knew me
or saw me then, so they wondered how do I recognize them
and what am I doing here?

Well, I told them I arrived here just a few days before
and I had family connections here before the war. My plans
were to live here and maybe begin to learn diamond cutting.
I got their names and talked to them. They invited me to their
house. The poor things, they lost their wife and mother and
they were starting to make women's underwear in a tiny
room of their apartment. I ended up living in Belgium for
five years and saw them frequently. We became quite good
friends.

The first thing they asked me was "How come you
didn't come over and ask us for food? We had so much food
we didn't know what to do with it." I said, "Well I didn't
expect anybody to give somebody any food for free. I mean
for some diamonds or gold? Or maybe something more
valuable or maybe for some cigarettes? But why would
someone get some for free?" They said, "We helped
everybody we could. We used to take all the leftovers in the
kitchen and share among people. You should have come
over and asked and we would have helped you."

Well, that is what happened. I could have been better
off and survived with much less difficulties than I did the last
few months. Hyme could have told me. He didn't have to
share. He could have just told me. Why not? You're a person
and you're a Jewish guy and you want to help your own
people whether you want to help anybody. He could have
said, "You know there's some guys over there, you go over
there and you ask them and they'll give you some soup."
Once we were liberated, I never saw Hyme again. I heard he
settled in France.

It's something that I still think about once in a while. I
am getting older and thinking about how people are and
human nature. Some people are always very kind and very
thoughtful. I wish I knew the name of the two French

128

people, father and son. I knew at the time I was in Belgium. God bless them. Wonderful people. I have always believed that people are good, and sometimes, you have to come to the conclusion that while most people are good, some are not.

THE LIBERATION

The Russians were coming. The Americans were coming. We saw American planes flying like little, tiny toys, hundreds of them in the sky. Both, from one side to the other. The Germans said whoever arrived first would kill us all. It was May 4, 1945.

Prior to this, the Germans had changed their style a few weeks before the end of the war, because they were being inspected by Geneva. They posted rules for treating prisoners equally and no one could be executed without central authority. In April, we hadn't been working in a couple of weeks, as the factory was at a standstill. The SS had been given last-minute orders to kill all of the prisoners in the concentration camps. They did in some places, but they decided we were going to go in and march. This was a dangerous area and we were going to be on the front lines. They told us that tomorrow we would be marching and be prepared to take a blanket and whatever water you have. A dish and a spoon was all we had.

We lined up at 4 a.m. and the SS took all of our belongings and gave us a loaf of bread and some margarine. The SS men took their possessions, such as bicycles and suitcases and made us carry their things. After hours of marching, we came to a wooded area in the Steyr forest, with beautiful surroundings and a stream at the bottom of a hill. At the top, there was a mammoth cave inside the mountain, and it was written in German that it was an air raid shelter. There was a very wide door and they marched us in, where we were sure to be executed. There were about 6,000 of us in the whole group, but maybe just 200 to 300 at that spot, and maybe 100 of us went inside. We said, "Where are the others?" Then somebody started to say it was a dangerous place to be. "Let's get out of here," one said. There were two exits. We went to one and the SS toting rifles and bayonets would not let us through, so we went to the other exit, and that group of SS did not resist, so we exited.

It was May 5, 1945. You could see the daylight. It was the most beautiful day – and the SS didn't resist. They let us out, so we went. No resistance. No one shot. They feared for their own lives a little.

We walked out and we had a picnic with our buddies. The first prisoner was left behind to bring some food for us. We had a lot of bread, margarine and sat on blankets. So we sat there. We felt it was a wonderful thing to have all that food. We were so happy because we could see and smell the freedom. You could just feel it. It was a wonderful feeling. Not so much that we will be free, but that the enemy would be destroyed. That was our concern, our hope.

Unexpectedly, one who was a lager at that point (a Polish guy) came out from the ravine. He was just coming up, as he had stayed behind. He was supposed to bring some lunch or soup. He walks in almost breathless and huffing in Polish, "Gentlemen, gentlemen, we are liberated! We are liberated! The Americans are back in the camp. We won the war back!" He was looking for the lagerfeld chief who was with us, walks over and they have a conference.

"The Americans are in the camp. They want us all back. We will go back to the camp and then we are free! Everybody line up!"

Back to the camp we went. As we were walking back, it was terrible because some of us couldn't walk. I was fortunate as I managed to walk, and together with one of the other guys, we helped carry each other. Just like a scene in a movie, we were dragging our feet. As we got closer, the right side was a stream lined with SS holding guns, and we walked on the left side by the factories. The path was so narrow, we had to walk one-by-one.

Then a miracle appeared: from about a 50 to 100-foot stack of iron and a bright sky above, a man walks out in a black uniform. Like a railroad man with a machine gun. I had never seen an American. He spoke perfect German and he ordered all of the Nazis to give up their weapons. They all became chicken and threw their guns. Some of us were going to grab the guns, but not me. I was a kid. The German prisoners were the first ones to grab the guns. It was a unique situation. A friend of mine, Rudy, he was a lawyer holding up a machine gun. I wish I could have taken a picture of that.

Then two hours later, a Jeep came with four G.I.s. What a feeling. They walked all the SS into the camp and there were some shots fired. I did not see it, but supposedly, there were two men from the SS killed as an example. The Americans discouraged us from retaliating against the SS, but the Russian, Ukrainian and other prisoners beat and killed SS or kapos who had treated them viciously, as an "eye for an eye." The Americans went to the barracks and they took everybody to the place they gathered the prisoners and there was a complete exchange with the SS. I didn't get a chance to talk to the American soldiers, because there were thousands of people surrounding us. They gave us chocolate bars and then we were free.

The United States Third Army, commanded by General George S. Patton, liberated five concentration camps: Buchenwald, Dachau, Dora-Mittelbau, Flossenbürg and Mauthausen. These first four camps were liberated April 1945 and Mauthausen was the last to be liberated on May 5, 1945.

I could walk out. I was a free man.

I went to the hospital to thank Kaufman and tell him goodbye. Kaufman was to me just like Schindler, a marvelous man. Kaufman was sitting in his office and next to him is a SS in the uniform of a prisoner. That SS man used to come to the barrack when I was there and I was an orderly – he would come count us twice a day. I never talked to this

SS and he never acted up. I shook his hand and I shook Kaufman's. I mean, why not? If he is with Kaufman, he is a human being and he protected him.

An American tank rolls down the main street of the Mauthausen concentration camp. [*May 5, 1945. United States Holocaust Memorial Museum, courtesy of Albert Abramson.*]

Kaufman tells me, "Franz, there are sick people left over in the basement of the factory who couldn't march and they need to be brought back to the hospital." They assigned a truck, another person and me. There were maybe a handful: six, eight or 10 people. They were lying down in the water. I remember many steps and it was pouring rain all night. I brought those people, some of them unconscious and I stayed all night, helping at the hospital. It was a very wonderful feeling that I could do something for Kaufman to repay him for his kindness.

The next day, I walked out of camp and never looked back.

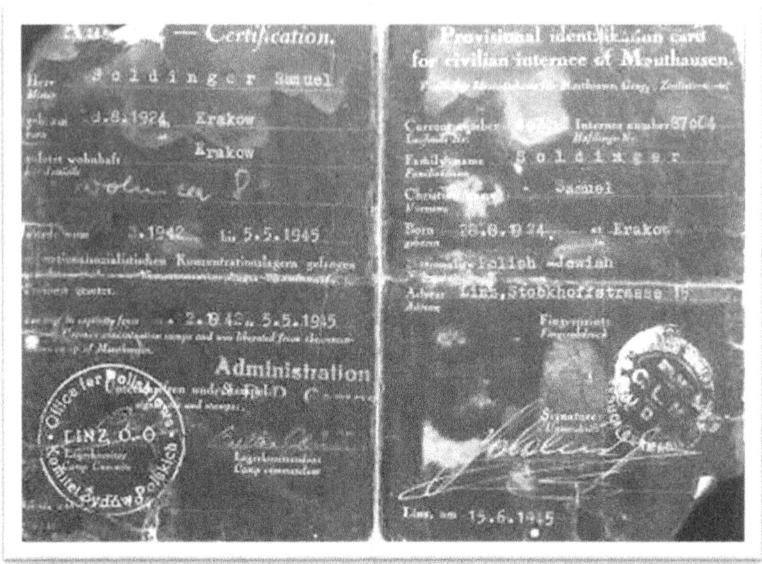

Liberation document from Mauthausen Concentration Camp

As told by reporter Max McQueen who interviewed Sam for an article in Arizona's Mesa Tribune February 4, 2001:

"Sam paused in retelling this story of revisiting Kaufman and carrying people in the rain, when he could have been free. A look came across Sam's face, as if for the first time, he understood the magnitude of his actions on that May day in 1945. A lone tear made its way down Sam's right cheek.

'I guess I did some good after all.'

Yes you did Sam, yes you did."

AFTER THE WAR

We were out.

I said to my friends Carl Braunhut and Chaim Friedner, "Where do we go now?" Like so many Jews who did survive, we had no one to go home to. We decided to go back home to Krakow -- which was about 500 miles -- and we were going to walk. We didn't get very far, because out on the street, we were surrounded by the townspeople and they all wanted to know how we are. They had heard rumors, but knew very little. One of the three of us was born in Germany, so they were excited they could speak with him in their own language.

After a while, the G.I.s were looting stores, so we got sugar and something to eat. Then we were invited by a lady, a nurse, to spend the night. My two friends stayed with her. Across the way, was the man who was the postmaster of Linz. He was an older man who had lost his wife, who died in a bombing. His daughter was in the country. So I went and sat all night with him and he was so inquisitive about what happened to us. He found a bottle of whiskey he had been saving until Hitler was overthrown and we drank all night. Like slivovitz. Imagine my stomach drinking whiskey, but it probably helped me.

Slivovitz was distilled in large quantities in Poland before WWII. A popular Passover alcohol, slivovitz had a strong standing among traditional Orthodox Jews in Krakow.

That was my first night over there and I stayed a few nights. We fetched pails of wine, filled bottles, and gave them to any American soldier who passed. We stayed in Linz a few days, but food was very scarce. You had to be like beggars and go to the hospital to get some food. It wasn't easy. I didn't know where to go. I did return to Krakow, but there wasn't anything or anyone there for me. A few weeks later, I decided to go to Palestine, then I went to another town in Germany then to Southwark, and from Southwark, I went to Italy.

After the liberation, Samuel (far right) and his fellow mates protested the conditions of the Bindermichl displaced persons camp in Linz, Austria.

I was in Italy and I found my uncle was searching for me. Every G.I. I met, I gave them more or less the address of my uncle in New York. This is how I made contact. I went back to Austria and made contact with my uncle, my father's brother, a wonderful man.

G.I. mail was the only way you could write. I had to travel to a small town in Austria and met the postmaster whose father was a friend of my uncle in America. Back through the G.I. mail, my uncle wrote me and suggested I go to Belgium so I could do something with my life. I kept asking people, "How do I get to Belgium?" I couldn't get a passport yet, no one could. The war is over. Everything was wild. Here comes another miracle.

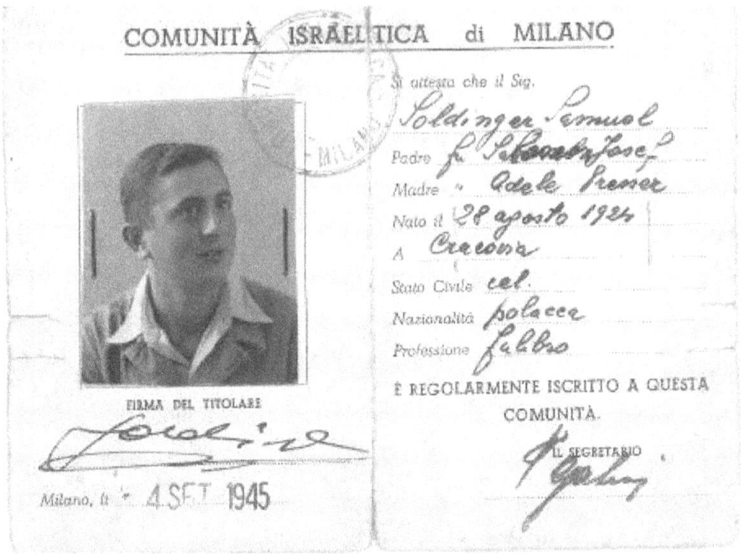

Passport 1945

A fellow by the name of Rosenstock, who was a G.I. and an English sergeant, came when he found out his brother is alive from the camps. He brought a uniform to take to his brother, but his brother was getting married when he arrived. I met him at the wedding, as I knew the brother and the bride before the war. I go to him and ask, "How can I go to Belgium?" I didn't know he had brought a uniform and he pointed at a bundle on the floor. "Why don't you try it on?" I became an instant sergeant.

I traveled with him to Belgium for seven days. I could not speak a word of English. It was terrible. People use to ask me, because I was tan, if I was from Israel and he told them I was.

We were sitting along the Champs-Élysées in France in the Officers Club, as he planned to meet some other guys who planned to go to Paris. I went with him wherever he went. I was sitting there with a couple of soldiers and they

138

left me alone in a booth. On my left, was a captain in the Polish army. He asked me if I had a watch. When I was in Italy in a citizen camp, somehow I got an old watch. They gave us some money there and I bought this old watch. He asked me what time it was and I held out my wrist to show him. He said thank you. I couldn't tell him the time, as I didn't want to give away that I couldn't speak English and wasn't a G.I.

Sam in his G.I. uniform

These photos include Ben Friedman,
Sam's best friend.

We landed in Antwerp, Belgium. This guy was scared because he had been stationed in Belgium. We ran through the tracks when the MP was coming. He brought papers. I had papers in my name, I was an English soldier. They must have stolen a book from the office. I went to the police and reported it. They were very gracious and gave me a permit to stay. There were a lot of people pro and con, but some people wanted to help the Jewish people. That is how I made it and stayed in Belgium.

I stayed in Belgium for five years. It took a long time until I got a permit to cut diamonds, with all the red tape. The Belgians rejected my permit on several occasions. Then, I gave my biography to one of the men in charge of the department of diamonds administration. He was an older man who asked, "Do you have proof you were in concentration camps?" I showed him my tattoo. He told me, "Come back in two weeks." I did and I got the permit.

See, when somebody is an angel, they are an angel.

Sam after the war

Sam in Belgium

Sam horsing around with friends after the war.

Photos taken after the war of Sam with friends.

144

Sam enjoying happier times on a ski vacation with other survivors who became lifelong friends.

I started cutting diamonds and contacted my uncle, who helped me financially. Not generously, but adequately, so I managed to survive. Unfortunately, I couldn't go to America because I was Polish.

The year before, my uncle came from America to visit me in Belgium. Then later, tragedy, as his wife died and then he died. Now, I had no one to go to in America. I almost didn't come and was contemplating changing my occupation. I had my Visa. I was stalling and stalling. Finally, I got on a boat and came to American on July 8, 1950.

A postcard Sam saved from the S.S. Stratheden, the ocean liner he came to America on in 1950.

Sam second from left, pictured with the captain and others on the S.S. Stratheden.

I settled in New York to the disapproval of my relatives. I had two cousins who received me very coolly. After I sent all of my baggage, I received a telegram from the husband of my first cousin's uncle's daughter. It read that they considered my trip opportunistic. I bought my own tickets with my own money. I didn't come with a refugee group. I was 25 years old and cried like a little boy. How could they be so rude?

I stayed in America with another uncle and worked for his company for a while. After some time, we had a falling out. I believe it was a big misunderstanding and have always blamed myself. But there was no going back to him or to Europe.

In all, it ended up turning out very well for me in America. I began diamond cutting in New York and started doing piecework. I would buy diamonds individually, polish and cut them. While I never became a very wealthy man, I made a decent living. That same cousin who shunned me lost his fortune, came back to me, and asked for a loan for $20,000. See, some people think they can do anything in this world.

After the war, while trying to find family survivors, Sam's uncle, who migrated to the United States prior to the war, told Sam that he had a job for him in New York City cutting diamonds and he would be his sponsor for migration. Sam applied for a visa and began learning the diamond trade in Antwerp, Belgium. On July 8, 1950, five years after the war ended, Sam arrived in America. He was one of 80,000 Jews from displaced persons camps to be allowed to immigrate to the United States, while 136,000 immigrated to Israel by 1952. Sam became a naturalized American citizen on May 31, 1955, a little more than 10 years after the American Army had liberated him from Mauthausen.

Sam's U.S. Naturalization Certificate

Sam and co-workers at a diamond cutting facility.

Sam checking his work by looking at a
diamond through a loupe.

In 1951, Sam met and married Saralee Salzberg, a Brooklyn native, and they went on to have three children: David, Adam and Laura.

Sam and Saralee in Brooklyn, New York

150

Saralee and Sam with sons David and Adam in
Brooklyn, New York

HARRY WINSTON AND DIAMONDS IN THE DESERT

I was cutting diamonds for a few years in New York. In the beginning, it was not easy. I was struggling, but I did become a good diamond cutter. After 12 years in New York, I was looking for an opening. I asked a friend who worked for Harry Winston if he knew of any jobs in the company. My friend said there was one he knew of!

I scheduled the interview, closed up shop for the day and got myself a fresh shave and new suit. I interviewed directly with Harry Winston himself. Meeting him was such an honor and he was very kind. He handed me a very large diamond and asked if I could cut it. I said, "Of course!" being confident in my abilities, but hopefully, not off-putting. The process of cutting a diamond was the same, regardless of the size of the stone. Then he asked to see my tattoo from the Holocaust, which I showed him.

Lo and behold, he offered me the job. But what was the job, exactly?

Harry Winston was a well-known jeweler at the time in 1963 in New York City. His diamonds were in high demand around the world and were often worn on red carpets by celebrities. He was known as the "King of Diamonds" and was the world's largest diamond merchant. Winston controlled every facet of wholesale and retail in the diamond industry.

Yet, the idea of this special job opportunity he had for me originated with someone else. That someone was the legendary Arizona Senator Barry Goldwater. See, Senator Goldwater had approached Winston with his concern about the chronic underemployment of people living on Arizona's Indian reservations. He told Winston that many of the Native Americans were fantastic jewelers and were good with working with their hands. They were patient and detail oriented. Wouldn't they make good diamond cutters, given the proper training? Winston thought they might.

My job was to handle this specific task of building and operating a new factory in Arizona and teaching the craft of diamond cutting to the workers. Harry chose me and had faith in me, because he figured if I survived the Holocaust, I would be empathetic to the plight of the Native Americans. I reported directly to Harry and I was very lucky to have this wonderful opportunity.

Sam Soldinger, top row, center; with Arizona dignitaries and Chandler leaders. *Arizona Daily Star* January 18, 1965.

Diamond Cutting Comes To Arizona

Editor's Note: Probably few Arizonans know that the renowned diamond expert, Harry Winston of New York City, has many of his gems cut in Arizona. The following story is from Arizona Public Service Co.'s publication, Spark and Flame.

Up until a year ago, if you told someone there were diamonds in Arizona, you might be taken for a fast-buck swindler trying to sell an acre of sand to a dude.

But today there are diamonds in Arizona. Thousands of them. They come to the state as dull, oddly-shaped crystals. They leave as brightly faceted stones for fine jewelry.

The reason is Harry Winston Minerals of Chandler.

Harry Winston is the world's largest diamond merchant. From headquarters in New York, Winston directs an operation that involves every phase of the retail and wholesale diamond industry.

Winston diamonds are cut in New York, Amsterdam, Antwerp, France, West Germany, Israel, and Puerto Rico. Each location has a capability for a particular size or type of stone.

In 1962, "King of Diamonds" Harry Winston negotiated with the U. S. Bureau of Indian Affairs. Would Winston be willing to locate a diamond cutting plant between the Salt and Gila Indian Reservations, and teach Papago, Pima and Apache Indians the painstaking craft?

Winston wanted to do what he believed was best for this country. The Indians would benefit by learning skills that would improve their standard of living.

Winston said yes.

Today, 15 Indian apprentices are learning to cut and facet diamonds.

The operation is fascinating. The raw diamonds are marked for cutting and are graded. Then they're carefully mounted and cut into two stones, one slightly larger than the other.

The stones are then girdled to make them perfectly round. Finally, in 58 separate operations, 58 facets are patiently ground to give each stone its peak brilliance.

There are no automatic machines — no electronic measuring devices — to indicate when each facet is perfect. Only a trained eye can see when too much or too little of the gem has been removed. A worker grinds and inspects, grinds and inspects, grinds and inspects, until he's sure the cut is right.

It takes three years to learn the trade. Obviously the training can be expensive in terms of possible spoilage.

The plant's manager, Samuel Soldinger, explains the operation this way: "It's not just cutting diamonds, but getting value out of the stone. Sometimes you can take a poor stone and improve it by careful cutting."

"Indians are shy, and they keep to themselves," Soldinger explains. "If they have personal or financial problems, they don't tell anyone."

Soldinger makes every effort to help out when there's trouble, and keep his workers happy. He makes it more than just good business practice. He takes a genuine interest in his employes.

As the Indians' skills increase, Soldinger believes his plant will be able to cut larger stones, where the margin of error is more critical.

"We're cutting diamonds here in Arizona that are sold all over the world," Soldinger says. "Maybe you'll buy jewelry made with our stones. They're as good as you can buy anywhere."

Arizona Daily Star January 18, 1965.

154

Arizona Indians cut diamonds at Chandler plant. This is the girdling operation.   PHOTOGRAPHS RALPH CANFIELD

Indians Cut Diamonds At Chandler Plant

Smocked reservation natives hunch over scientific
machines to prepare stones for milady's adornment

by Ralph Mahoney

Lillian Flores, 14-year-old Pima of Octillo, cuts diamonds.

AGRICULTURALLY-conscious Chandler has become the site of one of the most fascinating industrial operations west of the Mississippi.

Inside an inconspicuous 6,240 - foot - square building 83 Arizona Indians, whose forebears once picked cotton in the surrounding fields, are cutting diamonds for the commercial markets of America.

While diamond cutting is even more ancient than the Flemish cutter Van Berquem who discovered in 1475 that the hardest known substance in the world could be "faceted," the fact that it is being done by Indians gives it a special significance. Asiatic lapidaries long before the time of Van Berquem found that one diamond ground against another caused both stones to glisten.

HARRY WINSTON Minerals of Arizona began on a small scale toward the end of 1962 with four diamond experts from New York forming the nucleus around which the plant was built and around which it continues to flourish. The four were the instructors.

Harry Winston of New York, sometimes called "King of Diamonds," negotiated through his Arizona emissaries with the Branch of Employment Assistance of the Bureau of Indian Affairs. The idea was to provide employment for the residents of Arizona's Indian reservations and thus pump some economic stability into the reservations.

The site was selected because it is between the Salt and Gila reservations, both of which have a wealth of unskilled but trainable labor. The tribes represented are Papago, Pima, Apache and Navajo (one boy).

VICTOR J. Swanick of the Phoenix Indian Affairs area office and a vocational guidance expert is chiefly responsible for recruitment. The normal train-

—turn next page

Arizona Days and Ways Magazine May 10, 1964.

155

Diamond cutting and polishing is more than a job. It is an art. Only a genuine craftsman with a special feeling for his task can prove satisfactory in this fascinating industrial operation. It is intricate and precise and a worker must have infinite patience. He must develop a trained eye. We grind and inspect our work through a magnifying glass known as a loupe. Then we grind and inspect again. We repeat this process until it is just right. It takes a special person to have the patience, dexterity and eye to be successful.

I also very much enjoyed working in Chandler, which was a farming community and growing city east of Phoenix. I was quite involved in the Chandler Chamber of Commerce and once served as president.

Sam inspecting diamonds of his cutters at the Harry Winston Diamond Plant in Chandler, Arizona.

The following photos were taken at the Harry Winston Diamond Plant in Chandler, Arizona and shows workers cutting different facets of diamonds.

Sam with some of his factory workers.

Sam with off duty Chandler Police who provided
security for the Diamond Plant.

Sam and son Adam who worked at the Diamond
Plant during his teen years.

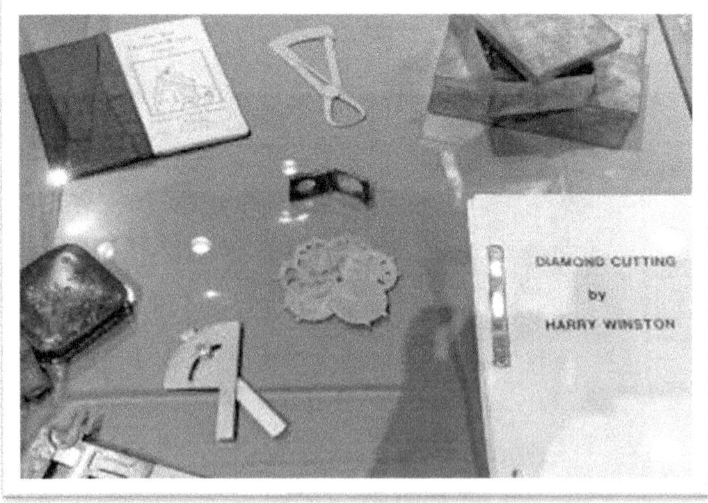

Diamond cutting tools and training materials.

162

ABOUT HARRY WINSTON

Harry Winston

Harry Winston was an American jeweler and known by many as the "King of Diamonds," a moniker bestowed on him by Cosmopolitan magazine in 1947. As the son of Jewish immigrants from Ukraine, Winston was born in New York, New York on March 1, 1896. At an early age, he was introduced to his father's jewelry shop and went on to start his own business in 1920 and opened his first store in 1932. Developing a reputation as a purveyor of extraordinary gems and creating innovative designs, Winston became the jeweler to movie stars, celebrities and royal families.

Debeers, a major diamond supplier in the world, sold most of its most important rough diamonds to Winston. Perhaps one of his most famous acquisitions was the Hope Diamond at 45.52 carats with a much-admired, beautiful deep blue hue. After owning and touring it for nearly 10 years, Winston donated the Hope Diamond to the Smithsonian National Museum of Natural History in 1958. In sending it to the museum, he shipped it registered first-class mail by the U.S. Postal Service in a brown envelope. After enjoying a storied career, Winston died in New York on December 8, 1978. Today, Harry Winston, Inc. remains committed to this form of creativity, rarity and quality in retail locations around the world.

ABOUT THE HARRY WINSTON DIAMOND PLANT IN CHANDLER, ARIZONA

Diamond plant during construction.

Diamond plant with mature trees.

Arizona Senator Barry Goldwater facilitated a deal between Harry Winston and the Bureau of Indian Affairs (BIA). The BIA would provide half of the funding for the

Native Americans to learn the diamond cutting trade in a factory built by Winston in Arizona. Trainees earned $1.25 an hour and training would take three years. Winston paid the diamond cutters and they would be eligible for raises based on their work.

Why did the process of training diamond cutters take so long? Cutting diamonds was done entirely by hand at the time. Cutting, polishing, faceting – every step of the process was done manually. For example, the final step in the process for many stones was to conduct 58 separate operations in order to create the 58 facets that would give a diamond its brilliant sparkle. Learning each one of these operations took time.

Winston hired a Chandler architect, Glenn McCollum, to design the plant. McCollum was a prolific architect, having designed hundreds of buildings around Phoenix at the time, from schools to churches, city halls, shopping centers and industrial buildings.

In 1963, Sam arrived in Chandler to manage this new diamond processing plant, Harry Winston Minerals of Arizona, Inc. It was 6,200 square feet, located on California Street (now Iowa Street) and Pecos Roads. It still stands today and is used by the Chandler Police Department as their evidence storage facility.

The plant got much attention for a number of reasons. Chandler was a small farm community where agriculture was the driving force in the economy and the Winston plant helped usher in a new phase of modern development and tech industries. It was the only diamond cutting plant west of the Mississippi River and the quality of Harry Winston diamonds were well known.

The professional workforce of the plant was also unique, being made up entirely of Native Americans, employing nearly 100 Native American cutters. While a few Chandler residents found employment at the diamond plant as security guards, clerks or secretaries, the majority of the workforce was Native American from local reservations. More than 80 percent of the employees were Pima, from the Gila River and Salt River reservations. Chandler was selected for the location of the plant, due to its proximity between the two reservations. The remaining 20 percent of the Native American workforce was Papago, Apache and Navajo.

Sam lauded the Native Americans and optimistically looked forward to the day when they would be cutting larger stones in the plant, stones where the margin of error shrank to nearly nothing. In the meantime, on any given day, there were some 2,000 stones in the plant. At the end of each day, every stone had to be accounted for, placed in long trays, and stored in a secure vault. The vault, Sam joked, had a burglar alarm that would go off at the drop of a diamond.

In a 1965 article in Tucson, Sam heaped praise on his employees, although at the same time, there were challenges. A BIA official lamented the turnover in the plant's workforce, yet still praised Sam for his management skills, being in awe of Sam's patience and supportive nature. Sam was always quick with a joke to bring a smile to his employees' faces.

Sam acknowledged that turnover was a problem, but he always took a position of understanding. One instance he cited involved an Apache in his first days on the job, learning the ropes from a Pima. The Apache quit, saying he couldn't take orders from a Pima. Such tribal rivalries were a common reason at the time for turnover in the workforce. Sam recalled that oftentimes at the end of the day on Friday, with a pocket full of wages, some of his employees would go out for a night on the town. On such occasions, when his employees may have found themselves arrested or sleeping off their excesses in jail, Sam would go to the courthouse and vouch for them in order to get them out. In one small sense, he was giving his employees the helping, generous nurturing that Schindler had extended to him in Krakow.

Harry Winston was right. Sam Soldinger was the right person for the job. It helped that Sam had a sunny disposition, despite his life experiences. He always maintained a positive outlook and was determined to help people and see the positive side of life.

Sam worked at the Winston plant in Chandler for 20 years until it closed in 1982. The company gave Sam the opportunity to continue working by moving back to New York City or heading to China to train the company's growing workforce. Instead, Sam decided to retire from Winston. He continued designing and selling jewelry from a small business he ran from his Phoenix home until his passing in 2001.

Q&A: ASKING SAM

Sam shows his Holocaust tattoo to one of his event guests.

The movie "Schindler's List" created a lot of buzz and interest in the Holocaust, and people wanted to know more. Sam was in high demand for speaking engagements and spent his retirement sharing his story of survival to audiences across the United States. During these speeches and press interviews, he always received many questions. Here is a sample and what Sam had to say:

How long did it take to tell your story?

When I first came to America, my English was limited. I tried to convey my story to people in New York and my distant relatives. Very few were interested. Now, after seeing "Schindler's List," people are interested in the story. That is a good thing.

Why did you survive?

I think it was God's will. It was just unbelievable. I was very lucky. Many times, my survival was a roll of the dice. For anyone who survived it, it's a miracle.

I had mechanical skills and training, which saved my life on more than one occasion. I had the support of good friends and family, which was a combination of compassion and willingness to take risks. When my cousin and I were working together in Schindler's machine factory, he told me "If you have to risk your life, only do it if you see that it's the end. Otherwise, don't risk it." Those words served me well.

I also believe I survived to tell my story, so people will learn the personal, not only the institutional story of the Holocaust. I speak about my experiences for Schindler and for the people who know how horrible World War II really was. I am not a psychologist, so I cannot say why some survivors are unable or unwilling to tell their stories. Before long, there will be no more survivors. We must publish our stories while they can be told from first person perspective. Every survivor has a story. Perhaps I had it easier than most. Of course, the ones who didn't survive couldn't tell their story. There are many who suffered throughout the war and didn't make it in the end. I can't speak for all these people. I wish I could.

Aside from the obvious, what do you believe Holocaust survivors have in common?

Those of us who survived the Holocaust have many things in common, one of which was the ability to adapt to conditions, no matter how horrific. Every survivor has a story.

How did Hitler's rise affect you?

My mother would worry about the future. There were rumors from Germany. In 1938, they deported the Polish Jews from Germany.

To survive, it seems you would have to take in everything that was going on around you, but then pretending like you didn't know anything either?

Well, no. We were just like on a checkerboard. They could dispose of you. My way of thinking was as long as they need me, they were going to keep me. I made myself useful. You're right, I pretended in some ways, and I was very lucky.

It seems like the Nazis would have killed Schindler for helping the Jews. Why did they kind of treat him with white gloves?

This part I don't know much about, except for what I am reading, just like you. I can't tell you because I wasn't there. See, what I am telling you about Schindler and my other stories are my personal experiences.

Did you see the gas chambers or crematoriums at Mauthausen:

We lined up by the bathhouse, but it was hot inside and I didn't see them. We didn't know for sure, but we heard they were there. I couldn't go and observe. Let's face it, once a building is a bathhouse, it's a crematorium. It was a giant building with several stories. The first structure was a kitchen.

Do you think this can happen again?

I don't think it will happen again in Germany, as they are ashamed of their elders. It could happen anywhere though. Maybe here in the U.S.? Maybe not against the Jews, but it could happen again against a different group. That is why, regardless of creed, we should all be united in love for one another. I can't stand it when I see discrimination, like what happened in Oklahoma City (Timothy McVeigh 1995) or what is going on in Bosnia (1994). It is the most horrible thing. I pray it will never happen again. There is a beautiful world out there and everybody deserves to live their lives. We shouldn't have any atrocities. The same forces that gave rise to Nazi Germany are operating in the world today. Each new generation should be vigilant.

Do you have any sustaining physical injuries from the Holocaust?

I had rheumatic fever during most of my time in the camps. I was very fortunate that I managed to survive the war. Due to the rheumatic fever, after the war, I developed heart issues. Consequently, in 1982, I went to Houston to have open-heart surgery, and in 1993, had another surgery to replace my heart valves, both because of the rheumatic fever long ago. Therefore, I am a healthy man as long as they last. Everything has its time, but I had very major surgeries.

Do you have any advice on how to handle mean people or bullies?

Try to be aware of the people who are against you. There are people who are not normal and try to create a hostile atmosphere. I am just hoping this will never happen again. However, you have to be aware of the fact that some people are cruel. In everyday life, don't be naïve. Don't be cheated by anyone. If you are naïve, someone will take advantage of you. Stay away from bullies and resist becoming a follower or one of them. Learn to think for yourself. While we can't all be leaders, we shouldn't all be followers either.

Did you ever have a crisis with faith?

We can't complain about the Almighty. I am not a religious person. Life to me is to be a good person. To help your fellow brother whenever you can. That is my philosophy. I came from a very religious family. My grandfathers had the beards. They prayed all the time. Then they all perished. I do not blame God. I believe in God. I worship God.

Do you have any pictures growing up or from that time?

When the SS found pictures, people got beatings, so I threw mine away. Can you believe it, I don't have a picture of me, how I looked as a child, from before the war started? I was lucky, when I was back in Poland after the war, I got a photo of my sister and my brother from their friends. I got a picture of my parents from my uncle in the United States.

Did you ever go back to Poland? How do you feel about the United States?

I went back to Poland in December 1945. I didn't see any members of my family. I was arrested three times for not being in the Polish army. I escaped from Poland and never went back. In later years, I did visit Israel four times. I saw Schindler's tree, but I didn't see his grave. I didn't go back to Poland, or visit the camps or the museum. It would have been too much for me. I love to be in the United States. That is where I feel safe. I am very proud to live in the U.S., and along the way here, I learned what life was all about. If you happen to be brought up with the finest food and finest situations in the U.S., you don't know the contrast, like I know the contrast, so I appreciate this country.

We live in a great country and we should kiss the ground of this great country of ours. God bless America.

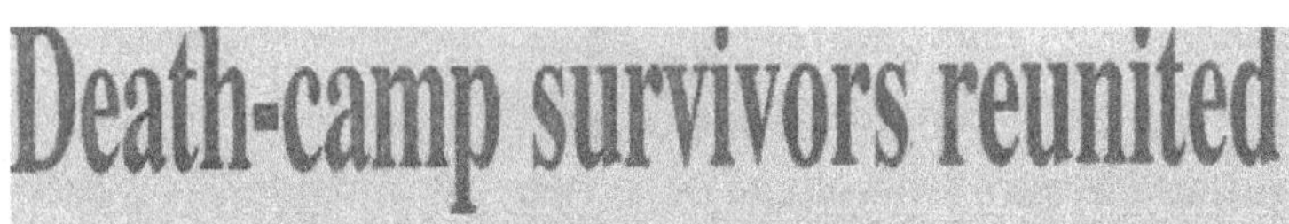

By Art Thomason
The Arizona Republic

They had grown close in the Mauthausen death camp during World War II.

Their lives were bonded as they shared the agony of brutal beatings. Their souls were fused by the horror of helplessness as loved ones were taken away and executed.

Hours before U.S. Army soldiers walked into the concentration camp in 1945 and liberated them, Sam Soldinger and Fred Friedner thought German SS officers were about to kill them.

But the American soldiers arrived and set them free.

More than 45 years ago, the two friends who had been through so much together walked through the gates of the death camp in Austria and parted ways. They hadn't seen each other since.

By a fluke, they were brought together again this week in Phoenix, where

— See DEATH-CAMP, page A9

Sam Soldinger keeps a picture of himself (right) and other concentration-camp prisoners that was taken after they were liberated from the Mauthausen death camp in 1945.

Victoria Buchanan / The Arizona Republic
A stroke of luck reunited Soldinger (left) and Fred Friedner, who parted ways more than 45 years ago, when they were freed from a concentration camp in Austria.

Arizona Republic March 30, 1991.

Death-camp survivors meet for 1st time since release

— DEATH-CAMP, *from page A1*

Soldinger now lives. A friend of his mentioned that he knew a man in San Francisco who originally was from Soldinger's hometown of Krakow, Poland. It turned out to be Friedner.

Luck, Soldinger said, has been one of their greatest allies for nearly a half-century.

"When I saw him at the (Sky Harbor International) airport, I jumped," Soldinger said, smiling warmly as he sat next to Friedner in his north Phoenix home.

"After all these years, I recognized him. We kissed and embraced. I hugged his wife."

For both of the Polish-born Jews, there are years of painful memories to recount. Memories of survival. Memories of tricking the German guards. Memories that spilled over, like wine, into Passover, the commemoration of the ancient Hebrews' deliverance from slavery in Egypt.

For two days this week, Soldinger and Friedner re-celebrated their own deliverance.

Both 66, the men grew up in Krakow, attending the same high school. They were 14 years old when war broke out and Adolf Hitler invaded Poland.

Each was assigned to ghettos, then to a series of concentration camps until both were taken to a concentration camp in Krakow. From there, they were condemned to Mauthausen, a complex of death camps.

After the war, Friedner moved to France, then to Belgium. Eight months ago, unbeknownst to Soldinger, Friedner came to the United States to live in San Francisco with his wife, Annie, and son, Andre.

"About a month ago, I was talking on the phone with my friend, Abraham Hirsch of San Francisco," Soldinger said. "He is a retired 5-and-10-cent-store owner. "We call each other periodically."

Hirsch said he had encountered a man from Soldinger's hometown.

"His name is Fred Friedner," Hirsch said. "I don't think you know him, do you?"

Excitedly, Soldinger replied, "What do you mean, I don't know him?"

As they sat Friday in Soldinger's living room, they talked of their efforts to survive the death camps and the belief that they might die only hours before the camp was liberated.

German guards herded them and other prisoners from the camp and its barracks up a mountain to a cavelike area. Soldinger and Friedner knew that American soldiers were getting close. Soviet troops were closing in from the other side.

"We thought they (German guards) were taking us up the mountain to shield us," Soldinger said. "Then they told us that they would kill us five minutes before the war ended."

Even though U.S. troops didn't arrive until hours later, prisoners had convinced some of the German guards that the end was close, and that they might as well lay down their arms.

At Mauthausen, Soldinger and Friedner tricked German officers into giving them jobs that provided a better chance for survival than most.

Soldinger and Friedner worked in an underground factory that manufactured German tanks.

"I was lucky," Soldinger said. "Because I worked there, I kept warm in the winter."

Friedner said he wanted no part of making machinery for the war effort, "so I played dumb, like I was stupid." He was assigned to a cleaning detail in the factory.

As they bunked next to each other in the filthy, lice-ridden barracks, they hunted extra food together, concocted schemes to fool the guards and strengthened each other's resolve.

"I lost my dear ones," Soldinger said. "He lost his dear ones."

Continued *Arizona Republic* March 30, 1991.

Oskar Schindler was a Nazi wheeler-dealer, an opportunist who used Jews as slave labor to provide the German Army with pots, pans, plates and fuse assemblies for anti-tank cannons.

Schindler pandered to and partied with military and Gestapo bigwigs in Krakow, Poland, while thousands of his Jewish workers were starved, tortured and killed by soldiers guarding the work camp adjacent to his factory.

Mention Schindler's name to Holocaust survivors Sam Soldinger and Arthur Rubinstein, however, and an air of respect and reverence engulfs them. With moist eyes, the two Phoenix-area residents say the same words:

"Schindler was a good man. He saved my life."

In truth, Schindler was a chameleon, pacifying his fellow Nazis on one hand, struggling to save the lives of his workers on the other. Arrested three times by the Gestapo, his bribes and political connections saved his life. In turn, Schindler saved 1,100 of his Jewish workers from extermination by having them classified "indispensable" to the German war effort.

The dramatic story is documented in director Steven Spielberg's three-hour, 15-minute epic film "Schindler's List," which opens in Tucson on Friday.

Following are the stories of Soldinger, 69, and Rubinstein, 75, who knew each other as children in Krakow, and who were lucky enough to have known Schindler and worked for him. Both were transferred to a labor and death camp in Austria in 1944, just before Schindler created his list.

At a time when brutality and death were the order of the day, both recognized and appreciated Schindler's concern and compassion.

Oskar Schindler on a holiday. Schindler gave this photo to Sam Soldinger, one of his workers during WWII.

The construction of Schindler's factory in Krakow, Poland.

The sweat dripping from young Sam Soldinger's brow on June 12, 1942, wasn't caused by just the heat in Krakow, Poland.

Its main cause was the two passport-like booklets the 17-year-old clutched in his hand. He was taking a chance that could get his whole family killed.

Two years earlier, the family had fled to Krakow from Warsaw's Jewish ghetto. Now, as the Gestapo's grip clamped ever tighter on the throat of Krakow's ghetto, groups of Jews were being rounded up and sent to death camps.

Sam knew wives still were allowed to remain with husbands, so he was trying to pass off his 46-year-old, widowed mother as his wife. Sam's sister's papers were included in his mother's booklet.

The man behind the table hardly glanced at Sam as he took the two booklets. Sam's papers showed he worked at the local airport, and thus was exempt from removal.

The man flipped through Sam's booklet and stamped it.

SCHINDLER, continued/3B

"You do not forget," said Arthur Rubinstein, a survivor of the Krakow, Poland, ghetto and several Nazi labor and death camps, sitting in the Phoenix living room of a fellow survivor.

"You keep things inside for 50 years, then a movie is made and it all comes back. I still can see my mother, my friends – they all were taken away. Since this has come up again, I can't sleep."

Rubinstein was a young civil engineer in Krakow when the German army went crashing across Poland's borders on Sept. 1, 1939.

"There were bombs falling, and no one knew what was going on," he said. "The Germans were in Krakow in just a few days."

Forced to work under the scrutiny of the invaders, Rubinstein and his two brothers saw the Krakow ghetto slowly destroyed.

"It was October of 1942 when they took my mother away," he recalled. "She was sent to Belzec, a sub-camp of Sobibor."

LIST, continued/3B

Standing behind the security bars at the Phoenix home of Sam Soldinger, Holocaust survivors Soldinger (right) and Arthur Rubinstein reflect the joy of survival and the pain of their memories. The men worked at Oskar Schindler's factory.

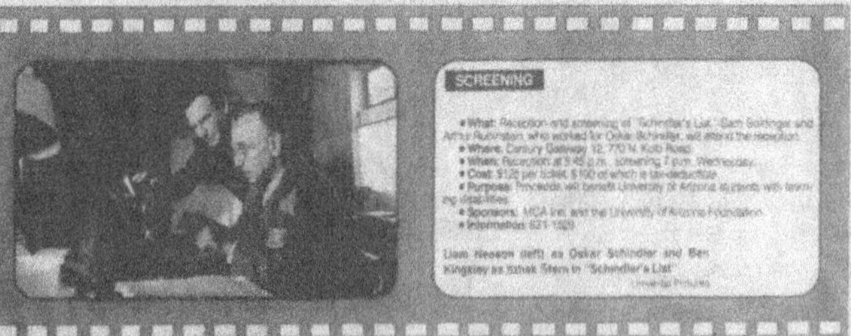

Liam Neeson (left) as Oskar Schindler and Ben Kingsley as Itzhak Stern in "Schindler's List."

Tucson Citizen January 10, 1994.

176

List saved some from death camps

Continued from 1B

the great extermination camp. We never saw her again. Later, in March of 1943, they liquidated the Krakow ghetto."

When the German troops finished their deadly work on March 13, 1943, more than 2,000 Polish Jews lay dead in the rubble of the ghetto. Thousands more had been rounded up and shipped away to various death and labor camps.

In June 1943, Rubinstein was sent to work at Oskar Schindler's plant, producing enamel plates and pots for the German army.

"At first, they would transport everyone to the plant each day," recalled Rubinstein. "But Schindler came up with the idea to make a camp right next to the factory. He wanted to get the people away from that other camp, where so many were being killed, and near his factory, where he could watch what was going on."

Although the camp where the Jews lived was under military control, by using bribes, suggestions and subtle pressure from his powerful Nazi contacts, Schindler kept conditions as comfortable as possible for his workers.

In August 1944, as the Russian armies continued to drive the Germans toward Poland, directives were handed down to relocate Schindler's plant farther to the west.

Part of his labor force was assigned that job. The rest, including Rubinstein and his brother Samuel, who was the camp doctor, were sent to Mauthausen, Austria.

"Schindler was angry that we were taken away from him, and was promised that he would get us back," Rubinstein said. "When he found out that wouldn't happen, he got furious. That's when he created his list."

Schindler had his remaining workers designated as "indispensable" to the war effort, and thus not subject to reassignment else-

where. That action saved 1,100 to 1,200 Jews from being sent to extermination camps.

In Austria, Rubinstein was assigned to procure steel girders to repair bridges hit by Allied bombing attacks.

"I would be working to order the girders and then I would suddenly be told, 'We don't need that bridge repaired anymore.'

"Then I would know that the area where that bridge was had been captured by the Americans. That way, we knew how far away the fighting was, and could figure out when we probably would be liberated."

Rubinstein's brother became a hero for many of the camp's ill and undernourished prisoners. He would hide them from guards and somehow secure medicine and supplies for them.

"Dr. Rubinstein was a saint," said fellow Holocaust survivor Sam Soldinger. "He saved my life when I was sick, and he saved lots of others lives, too."

Both of Rubinstein's brothers survived the war and now are retired in Florida.

After the war, Rubinstein came to the United States and resumed his career as an engineer. He and his wife, Alma, a survivor of the Auschwitz extermination camp, lived in several other countries before settling in Pasadena, Calif.

They moved to Sun City West in 1988. They have three grown children in California.

"Some memories will never go away," said Rubinstein. "For instance, something as simple as a triangle takes on tremendous importance for people like me. You see, the prisoners had to wear a triangle on their chest. A red triangle meant you were a political prisoner and a black triangle meant you were a criminal.

"But a yellow triangle," he said, tears filling his eyes, "a yellow triangle meant you were a Jew."

Schindler showed kindness, survivor says

Continued from 1B

Sam wouldn't be removed from Krakow. When the fellow flipped Sam's mother's booklet open and automatically stamped it, too, the teen-ager's heart leaped.

But then the man looked at the woman's picture again, glanced up at young Sam - and marked a big X across his mother's stamp.

It was a death sentence for Sam's mother and sister. They were taken away. He never saw them again. If the clerk had been angry, Sam too could have paid with his life.

For the next three years, Soldinger's luck and intuition saved his life time after time.

On Oct. 28, 1942, he was among 1,600 workers rounded up to be shipped away.

"A man was directing some people to the left and others to the right," Soldinger recalled last week during an interview in his Phoenix home.

"The smaller, weaker people were sent to the left. He ordered me to go right. Then I heard him say, 'We have enough. Everyone else go to the left.'

"They died, and we lived. It was all just luck," he said, shaking his head sadly, "... just luck."

Soldinger helped build barracks at the camp where he was sent. He quickly learned that challenging the guards was not wise.

"They ordered some of the people to go to another place," Soldinger recalled, "and the camp doctor turned to the guard and said, 'But you promised to keep me here!'

"The guard made him get undressed and lie on the ground at his feet. Then, he said, 'You're right. You will stay.'

"Then he shot him."

One night Soldinger was shaken awake and saw three SS officers standing by his bunk.

"'Electrician, you come with us!'" one of them snarled.

Instead of the firing squad he expected, Soldinger was led to the SS barracks, where the electricity had failed. His knowledge of electricity was limited to the basics, but Soldinger knew he would be killed if he told them that.

"I was shaking," he said. "Luckily, when I opened the fuse box, I found that a couple of the fuses were loose. I pretended to work for a while, then tightened the fuses and the lights came on. They thought I knew what I was doing. I overheard one of the SS men say, 'Can you believe that a Jew could figure out something like that?'"

When a call came for metal workers, Soldinger impulsively stepped forward, even though he had no metal work experience. That's how he ended up at Schindler's plant in Krakow.

"He greeted each new person individually, and asked several questions of each of us," Soldinger remembers. "You could tell he cared. He was very flashy - he always wore a big diamond ring."

Soldinger was the only Jew in the crew he was assigned to, and was shocked when he was promoted to foreman. The anti-Semitic feelings of the other slave laborers nearly cost him his life.

"They wouldn't do what I told them, so I ended up working like the devil, doing my job and much of theirs, but I couldn't keep up. I was told to make quota or go up against the wall and be shot. When the men still wouldn't help, I fought one of them, and we each got 10 lashes with a whip. Finally, they picked a new foreman, and things got better."

One evening Schindler approached Soldinger for a chat.

"He was kind and gentle," Soldinger recalled. "He asked me if I was a good swimmer, and I said I was. He looked into my eyes with kindness and said, 'It would be nice if you could swim across the ocean to America and escape all of this horror.'"

At one point, Soldinger was stricken with rheumatic fever. His Jewish friends carried him to work each day, then hid him under some papers so the guards wouldn't discover him. They would meet their own quotas and those of the sick people, too.

"If you were very sick, they would send you to the extermination camps," Soldinger explained.

On Aug. 6, 1944, Soldinger was transferred to Mauthausen, Austria, where he worked in a rock quarry with 280 steps carved into the side of the pit. If the rocks the Jewish workers hauled up the 280 steps were too small, he said, the guards' punishment was brutal.

They would push them off of the steps and they would fall to their deaths."

Later, Soldinger was moved to another Austrian camp, near Linz, that was liberated at war's end by U.S. Gen. George S. Patton's 3rd Army.

Soldinger later found Schindler living in squalor at a displaced persons camp.

"The Jews he had saved took care of him as best they could," Soldinger said. "I thanked him for saving my life."

Soldinger came to the United States in 1950. He became a diamond cutter and moved to Arizona in 1963. Divorced, he has two grown sons and a grown daughter.

"One thing I promised myself back then, when I couldn't change clothes for a year at a time, was that I would never be dirty again," he said.

"I keep myself clean, and my clothes are neat and clean.

"Always."

Continued *Tucson Citizen* January 10, 1994.

MORE THAN A MOVIE

Schindler's list saved Valley pair's lives

David Petkiewicz/The Arizona Republic

Sam Soldinger stands near a photograph of his parents. The Polish Jew will always recall the day he was chosen to go to the Krakow factory of Oskar Schindler, a process depicted in the current film *Schindler's List.*

Film event to honor survivors

By Carol Sowers
The Arizona Republic

By the time he was 18, Sam Soldinger had escaped death dozens of times.

"I had many close shaves," he said from his Phoenix home.

He had been lashed with a whip, beaten and nearly starved when he was forced to work for the Nazis as an electrician in a German-occupied airport in Krakow, Poland, during World War II.

But the day that will not leave him is Oct. 28, 1942, the "Selection Day" that would eventually lead Soldinger, a Polish Jew, to the factory of Oskar Schindler and to a temporary reprieve from the Nazi death camps.

Schindler, part-hero, part-flamboyant-entrepreneur, is the Nazi-

Sam Soldinger (far right, holding up sign) poses with other survivors of the Mauthausen concentration camp, where he toiled in a tank factory.

turned-Jewish sympathizer who rescued Jews from almost sure liquidation in German death camps. The story of how Schindler used his influence to save Jews by employing them in his factory in Krakow is the subject of the award-winning movie *Schindler's List.*

The movie, directed by Steven Spielberg, is playing in Phoenix and around the country. The "list" refers to the names on a roster of 1,100 Jews who worked for Schindler.

On Oct. 28, 1942, Soldinger was

— See **SCHINDLER'S**, page A7

Arizona Republic January 12, 1994.

Schindler's list meant survival to 2 Valley men

— **SCHINDLER'S**, *from page A1*

already half-dead when the Gestapo came to the airport.

They ordered the 1,600 workers to line up while officers strode up and down, tapping with a whip those who were to go left — to the death camps — and those who would go right — to continue working at the airport.

Soldinger was ordered right.

In April 1943, the Gestapo returned, seeking more Jews for a death camp. But because Soldinger was an electrician, he was ordered to work in Schindler's munitions factory in Krakow. The factory also produced enamel pots and pans, according to the movie.

"We had never heard of Schindler," Soldinger said. "He came in beautifully dressed, a very charming man. He always had a cigarette in his hand. Without any screaming or yelling, he talked to each one of us, told us he was happy to have us with him."

The factory was "a resort" compared with the Nazi camps, remembers Arthur Rubenstein, 75, of Sun City, an engineer who also was ordered to work for Schindler in April 1943.

Working 15 hours a day, seven days a week, Schindler's "employees" slept in three-tiered bunks and lived on coffee substitute, bread and "weak soup," Rubenstein said.

Despite the bleak conditions, Rubenstein said, "we knew he was saving us."

Soldinger agreed that life was better in the factory, but he said he and others were beaten by Nazi guards when Schindler was not present.

"He wasn't there 24 hours a day," Soldinger said. "Nobody was beaten before Schindler's eyes. He was a perfect gentleman."

After 50 years, Soldinger remembers Schindler's tiny gestures that had huge significance for the factory workers.

"Schindler was always smoking, and he would take one or two puffs from a cigarette and drop it on the floor, so someone could pick it up," said Soldinger, who is now 68. "He also allowed some people to go to his garage and listen to the BBC at night."

By August 1944, Allied troops were pushing the Germans back into their homeland, and Schindler moved his factory from Poland to Czechoslovakia.

"He wanted to take all of us with him. He was like a father to us," Soldinger said. "But that was impossible."

Schindler could not save everyone, and many of his workers, including Soldinger and Rubenstein, were ordered to Mauthausen, a death camp in Austria, where they worked in a tank factory.

"It was a horrible place, no food,

Oskar Schindler gave Sam Soldinger this photo of himself. "He was like a father to us," Soldinger says today of the man who saved his life.

no hygiene, no water to bathe. We were starving," Soldinger said.

Almost a year after Soldinger and Rubenstein went to Mauthausen, on May 5, 1945, Gen. George Patton's 3d Army arrived to liberate the skeletal prisoners in the camp.

"I owe my life to Patton and Schindler," Soldinger said.

He and Rubenstein will recall Schindler and the dark days of the Nazi occupation when they are honored tonight prior to a special showing of the movie sponsored by the University of Arizona Foundation. A portion of the proceeds from the $125 tickets at the Century Gateway 12 Theater in Tucson will benefit the university's Strategic Alternatives Learning Techniques, a program for college-age learning-disabled students.

Rubenstein has not seen the movie, "fearing it would be too difficult."

He will see it tonight, however.

Rubenstein, who like Soldinger, lost relatives, including their mothers "to the ovens," said he does not savor the publicity he has received since the opening of the movie.

"But once they asked me to come to Tucson, I could not refuse," he said. "There are so many denying this ever happened. You cannot forget."

Soldinger, who has seen the movie, sobbed when the darkest days of his past flashed by him in the stark black and white Spielberg chose for the movie.

"I did not like to see the killing, but when I thought of my mother and sister (who died in the death camps), I cried," he said.

Continued *Arizona Republic* January 12, 1994.

TO SAM WITH LOVE

To my father, I cannot even imagine the terrible suffering you went through. I tremendously admire the courage you must have had. I constantly pray for your good health and that you live a long life to spend many years sharing your experience for the prosperity of mankind in the future.

David Soldinger
1995

David said this in a 1995 interview prior to Samuel's passing in 2001. David passed away in 2020.

In one's lifetime, we come across a few special people who make a lasting impression and influence on our lives.

In one's lifetime, we come across a few special people who have lived an incredible experience and we feel special because our lives were touched by their journey.

In one's lifetime, we become humbled, to the point of being absolutely in awe of someone's remarkable deed or true-life experience.

In one's lifetime, we are often reminded that what we thought were major problems are pale in the light of someone else's personal life and death struggle.

In one's lifetime, we read or hear about the genocide directed against the Indians, Asians, Jews, Muslims and so forth and we think that could never happen again.

In today's lifetime, we read about the atrocities in Sarajevo and believe that could not happen in America.

In today's lifetime, we read about the bombing of New York's World Trade Center and believe that could not happen in Phoenix, Arizona.

In today's lifetime, we Pledge Allegiance to the Flag and take for granted our freedom.

In 1994, I had the extreme honor of introducing Sam Soldinger, who spoke at our Phoenix Parks, Recreation and Library Department meeting. He changed my life with his miracle life story, along when I saw the depiction of Sam's horror-stricken young life in the movie "Schindler's List."

Dale Larsen
Assistant Director
City of Phoenix Parks & Recreation
March 10, 1994

182

Dear Mr. Soldinger,

I thank you for sharing your time and memories with us. Although we may never truly know the depth of your experiences, I felt the pain and the degradation inflicted upon you and many others. It is with sincere admiration and regard that I hold for you and all of the victims of this time.

I believe our students have a greater appreciation of history with the first-hand account you gave. Many have said that before this year, they did not know about the Holocaust. By educating our young people, perhaps we can hopefully demonstrate the importance of acceptance, and appreciation for our fellow man.

We <u>must</u> never forget. Your words of courage and hope will remain a part of all of us.

Sincerely,

Susan Soroka
A Phoenix elementary school teacher
May 18, 1994

Dear Sam Soldinger,

I just want to write you a short note of thanks. I want to tell you that I admire you and the way you dealt with the horrible things you have gone through. I think that a lot of times when people taste the bitterness of society, they tend to want to "get society back" for what happened. I think the fact you are speaking to us today shows what a humble, kind and loving person you are. I am truly sorry you had to go through all you did.

I think you have a really important story to share with others because the way you tell it touches all. I don't think I could ever fully relate with you about your experience, but I really am interested in understanding it. I traveled to Krakow, Poland, and Slovakia, Ukraine and Auschwitz. I saw the ghettos in Krakow, the camp in Auschwitz and the museum. The experience really affected me, and every time I think of it, a huge bubble of sorrow grows within my heart.

I would love to converse with you and hear more about your experience. Now, I write to let you know that I think your speaking will affect us more than you know. From hearing your story, I realize that so many of my problems are so small compared to what some people go through.

Thanks again for speaking. I really think you are a wonderful man.

Sincerely,

Anna Rampton
Crescent Valley High School
Corvallis, Oregon
April 25, 1995

Dear Mr. Soldinger,

In sharing your personal testimony as a survivor of the Holocaust, you have granted future generations the opportunity to experience a personal connection with history.

Your interview will be carefully preserved as an important part of the most comprehensive library of testimonies ever collected. Far into the future, people will be able to see a face, hear a voice, and observe a life, so that they may listen and learn, and always remember.

Thank you for your invaluable contribution, your strength and your generosity of spirit.

All my best,

Steven Spielberg
Chairman
Survivors of the Shoah
Visual History Foundation
March 4, 1996

Eulogy of Samuel Soldinger by Holocaust Historian Paul Wieser

Leann and I knew Sam for a number of years. I knew him well enough to know that he wouldn't want his memorial to be a somber occasion.

I also know that Sam would want me to mention a few very special people in his life. I know they were important to him because in many of our conversations he would repeatedly speak of them. His mother and father. His brother and sister. Oskar Schindler who saved his life. Harry Winston who gave him an opportunity to be successful when he first came to this country. And his pride and joy, the light of his eye, his daughter Laura.

In many ways, Sam was a private man. But I, as no doubt many of you, got to see another side of him: the gentle, caring, generous side. I have a number of fond memories of my knowing Sam and a few I would like to share briefly.

<u>My Wife Leeann's Ring</u>

It was fall '95 and the National Council for the Social Studies was holding their national convention in Phoenix. I was one of the organizers and I had put together a panel discussion that featured Sam with a few other scholars. We filled the hall with about 800 people and Sam was the hit of the show. It was right after the Schindler movie had come out, so interest was at a fever pitch. After the event, Sam suggested we go out for a bite to eat.

On the way over to Miracle Mile Deli at Park Central Mall, I told him that I was thinking about asking Leeann to marry me. He understood immediately what I was asking.

186

He placed his hand on my knee and said, "When it comes time I'll treat you like a brother."

The time eventually came and within a short period we found ourselves in the house of Sam Soldinger in his tiny office down the hall. I really thought that this was going to be something like a typical jewelry store: look at a bunch of rings and what you see in store windows at most malls. Well I was mistaken. Sam reaches down and opens a safe that was built into the floor. He spreads a velvet cloth on his desk and then spills out a pile of diamonds. It was as if he had summoned the stars from the heavens to fall to this one place. Sam finally broke the silence when he asked Leeann what she wanted. Leann then launches into this long explanation on settings and cuts and a few other details that I never knew existed. While she was going on and on, Sam patiently listened while he fiddled with things on his desk, arranging this and that, here and there. When she finally came to the end – and I'll never forget this – Sam said, "You don't want that."

Quickly realizing we were out of our league and that a rather long negotiation was about to break out, I simply said, "Sam, what *do* we want?" He then offered a rather overwhelming explanation of the flaws in Leeann's choices and in due course presented us with some outstanding alternatives. Thus, a ring was decided upon that very day. But that is not the end of the story. The ring has gone on to have a history of its own.

Oftentimes with work associated with the U.S. Holocaust Memorial Museum in Washington, D.C., I would take groups over to Israel, Poland, etc. Before traveling, I toured the group through the museum. At the Mauthausen exhibit, I always told stories about Samuel Soldinger. In his memory, I always touched one of the stones that is part of the exhibit. I always ended with the story of the ring. It was always extremely popular and moving at the same time, especially with the women. If the group was from Arizona, upon our return, Leeann would be waiting at the airport to pick me up. When the group learned who she was, she was immediately set upon; everyone wanted to see "the ring." Leeann knew I was telling that story again. The story took on a life of its own because within a year or two college students entering our programming mentioned that one of their professors had told that story in her class! She must have been a participant in a former program.

The Menorah

I bought this Menorah which was rather unique – the candle holders were small reproductions of synagogues that no longer exist. One is from Krakow. So one Christmas I had a bunch of former students over and invited Sam, who brought his grandson Paul. When it came time to light the candles I explained the significance of Hanukkah and how the Menorah fit in. We took turns lighting the candles and when we got to the Krakow Schul, Sam did the honors. We all had a wonderful time. I think Sam had the best time of all, but that was just the way he was.

The Shoah

I would be remiss if I did not address a subject that was of singular importance to Sam – that being the Shoah. To a historian who has spent a significant part of my life devoted to the study of this horrific period of time, Sam was a living link to a time that most can only wonder about and now belongs to history. A time when children played in the shadow of the Wawel Castle and on the crowded streets of the Kazimierz District of Krakow. Where peddlers hawked their wares, where bearded men rushed off to schul at Remah

Synagogue and where mothers made sure Saturday evening's meal was taken off to the bakers in time.

This way of life was suddenly ended by a hate the world had never experienced. A hate that would claim millions of lives and make lifetime victims of the handful of individuals that would survive. Sam would lose his mother, sister and brother to this hate.

It was in their memory that he spoke to countless audiences, both young and old, and told of victims, perpetrators and bystanders, and of the horrid effects of indifference, prejudice and discrimination. Never again was his simple message.

Sam's voice has now gone silent, but his message must never be allowed to do so. Sam would agree that if truth and reason are to prevail, we all must remain vigilant. The still, small voices of millions cry out to us from the ground demanding we do no less.

Shalom Sam.

Paul Wieser
Holocaust Historian and Teacher
Eulogy of Samuel Soldinger
Sinai Mortuary – Phoenix, Arizona
January 4, 2001
Sentiments added in 2021

Eulogy of Samuel Soldinger by Rabbi Michael Rovinsky

The Talmud tells us that when one of the great sages was about to depart this world, he told his trusted student to be sure to deliver a moving and stirring eulogy because he would be standing there listening. Why? What was so important that warranted a warning by the great sage that he would be listening to the eulogy that was being delivered about him.

To understand this incident recorded in the Talmud, we must first understand the purpose of a eulogy. Contrary to popular belief, the purpose of eulogizing a departed loved one, is not for the sake of glorifying the departed, but rather for our benefit. The purpose of a eulogy is to speak of the good and outstanding qualities and character traits possessed by the deceased so that we may learn from them, and be inspired to emulate those qualities in our own lives. Not only does this result in us becoming better individuals, but it allows the deceased to live on through us as we emulate the positive character traits of the deceased.

It is also noteworthy that the Hebrew word for eulogy, hesped, is written with the same letters as the Hebrew word hefsed, which means "loss". The message again being that the purpose of the hesped, the eulogy, is to realize what was lost as a result of the death of the individual and the need to fill the loss, to fill the void by emulating the special qualities of the deceased.

It is for this reason we have gathered to eulogize Sam Soldinger, Shmuel ben Shlomo, this afternoon. We, his family and friends, have come from all over to spend a brief period of time reviewing the life of Sam, so that we can earn and hopefully emulate his special qualities, thereby, enabling Sam to live on in each and every one of us.

190

Sam was very proud of his heritage. It didn't take long in one's first conversation with him to learn that he was born into a Chassidic family in Krakow Poland. Sam's childhood was stolen from him by the Nazi's, may their memory be erased, and when he was 14 he had to face the outbreak of WWII. Because of his tall size, Sam was able to land a job working at the Krakow Airport. Each morning he would leave the ghetto to do his job at the airport in a manner that would leave him enough time to try and obtain food, which he would smuggle back into the ghetto for his family. It was while working at the airport, that Sam met famous Mr. Schindler who took him to work in his factory. Eventually, the Nazis closed the factory and Sam was taken to the infamous concentration camp, Mauthausen.

After the war, Sam made his way to the United States, where he realized material success and was blessed with three children: Laura, David and Adam, and a grandson Paul whom he loved so dearly. I had the good fortune of meeting Sam in 1984 when I joined his extended family. And family was so important to Sam. Whenever we spoke, the first item on the agenda was his children, my children, their health, their accomplishments and anything that gave him nachas from the members of his family. Maybe he appreciated family so much because he knew what it was like to be without family, as he lost his family in the war. Education was also very important to Sam, and he constantly let us know how important it was. I vividly remember his words of encouragement during my years of yeshiva and college study.

Anyone who knew Sam couldn't help but notice the prominence he gave to and the eagerness with which he would share his experiences of the Holocaust to all who would listen. Some people might have been tempted to say enough already. It's over, get on with your life. But Sam knew better. He knew he was spared for a reason. That reason, first and foremost, was to rebuild that which had been lost so that it should never happen again. And I believe this outlook on life, which was infused and shaped by the war, served as the guiding force in all his actions.

Sam was extremely proud of his Jewish heritage and family background as mentioned earlier. I always found Sam to be a very generous and giving person. My son Avi and I were talking last night and he was relating his memories of how Sam met us in California on one of our vacations to take the children to Disneyland.

Next to his family, friends were of paramount importance to Sam. It says in "Ethics of the Fathers" that one should acquire for himself a friend. The word friend is in the singular. So our sages ask, "Why not many friends?" They answer, "Because a true good friend is so rare, that if we managed to have such friend in our lives, we have been truly blessed." Sam was blessed with many quality friends. He kept up with friends from his days in Krakow. I recently performed a bris in Dallas, and after the bris, a husband and wife came up to me and said they had been with Sam in Mauthausen and had maintained their friendship over these past 55 years. Sam took pride in his friends and his friendships with them. His friendships crossed generational lines. Not only did he relate to those his own age, but he was able to strike a chord with the friends of his children, to such an extent that they would always ask about his welfare and share little anecdotes with Laura about their encounters, whether at the lounge or buying a diamond. Sam made a lasting impression on all those who were fortunate enough to meet him.

In this week's Torah reading, when Yosef, after having been sold as a slave and lost from his brothers and father for 22 years, reveals himself to his brothers, the first thing he says is, "HaOd Avi Chai - is my father still alive?" Yosef was asking much more than if Jacob was still alive in the physical sense. Because physical existence is but a mere blink of an eye. Rather, Yosef was asking if the brothers were continuing the life of their father Jacob by emulating his ways. Yosef wanted to know if the brothers were living up to their obligation to follow the teachings of their father Jacob. This was the question of "HaOd Avi Chai - is my father still alive?" And this is the question each of us, especially Laura, David and Adam must ask ourselves today. HaOd Shmuel ben Shlomo chai? Is Sam Soldinger still alive? Are we prepared to incorporate into our lives the things that your father and our friend stood for? This is why Shmuel ben Shlomo, Sam is standing here at this moment listening to our eulogies. He wants to know if he made a difference in our lives. He needs to know that his personality, his very essence, his existence has affected us in a positive, motivating way. If each of us would pick just one character trait that we admired about Sam, then he will continue to live on through each of us and we will be a merit for his soul.

The custom is to request forgiveness from the deceased at this time. Therefore, on behalf of your family and friends, we request forgiveness.

There is one more custom we have when concluding a eulogy and that is to ask the deceased to go before God and beseech blessings for his family, friends and the entire Jewish people.

The story is told that when the Gerrer Rebbe came to visit the U.S. in 1998, there were thousands of people waiting in line to receive the blessing of the holy Rebbe. Realizing the difficulty placed on elderly people who were standing in line for long periods of time, those in charge quickly created a number system, giving each person a number indicating his or her turn to appear before the Rebbe. To ease the potential discomfort of the elderly, they allocated the numbers based on age, with the elderly receiving a lower number thus enabling them to enter first.

Unaware that a number system had been implemented, an elderly Jew walked up the steps and requested entry to see the Rebbe. The men at the door asked to see his number. So the elderly European immigrant rolled up his shirtsleeve and displayed the number that was tattooed on his arm when he arrived in Auschwitz. The man was immediately taken to see the Rebbe.

Sam, you lived a full but difficult life. You experienced things that we couldn't imagine in our worst nightmare and you are now on the way to meet the Almighty. Your experiences during the Holocaust have earned you the right to walk straight in and stand before God. So we ask you, Shmuel Ben Shlomo, Sam Soldinger, that when you arrive there, roll up your sleeve and show Him your holy numbers and then, in that merit, ask God to watch over and bless your beloved family and friends and to protect our people both in Israel and abroad.

Rabbi Michael Rovinsky
Eulogy of Samuel Soldinger
Sinai Mortuary – Phoenix, Arizona
January 4, 2001

Dear Laura,

To honor your dear father, Pam and I have ordered a paving stone in his memory to be placed on our Avenue of Angels. This paving stone will be engraved Samuel Soldinger and will be a permanent part of our Village. Many wonderful memories are born on this walkway, as thousands of families and visitors use this scenic and active area every day. This is our "Main Street" leading from the Gingerbread house to all the new attractions we have for the kids. This is a most fitting and marvelous way to remember Samuel's special life because you have been such a big part of our Give Kids The World family.

You will continue to be in our thoughts and especially in our prayers.

With love,

Henri Landwirth Pamela Landwirth
Chairman Emeritus President
Give Kids The World
Kissimmee, Florida
January 5, 2001

**Note Henri Landwirth was also a Holocaust survivor, Samuel's dear friend and best man in Samuel & Saralee's wedding. Mr. Landwirth passed away in 2018.*

Dear Mr. McQueen,

I just wanted to thank you for the tribute you wrote for the paper on February 4, 2001, following the death of Sam Soldinger. I was privileged to have gone to high school with Mr. Soldinger's daughter, Laura, and was so proud of her and her family when I read this article. She and I are still in contact today, almost 20 years later, and I can honestly say that Mr. Soldinger's character and strength live on vividly in Laura.

I didn't even know much of the information I read, not that I would have understood the impact of it when I was a teenager. So, I especially appreciate the honor you gave to the experiences Mr. Soldinger lived through. I can't fathom enduring such times, and appreciate learning of them and sharing them with my own children … doing what I can to make sure we work at never allowing such to take place again.

Again, thank you for writing such a wonderfully honoring tribute … one that truly brought tears to my eyes.

Mrs. Jessica Franks
February 20, 2001

"In the end, Sam lived well and free, a fitting foil to the Nazi's plan for him and all Jews."

Max McQueen
Tribune Newspapers
1994

Dear Laura,

I had teary eyes when I saw the photo of your father looking at a diamond with his jewelry loupe. He looked just like my father. I remember them both doing that together. They would spend hours opening up the little white envelopes where they kept the diamonds and look for quality, cut, etc.

Sam survived so many close calls and made himself an expert in many different fields to survive. What a brilliant man. We loved your dad so much like we love you! Thank you for sharing your life with us.

Lisa and Mike Katz
2021

My name is Tana Martin and I worked with Laura at the City of Phoenix when she was in aquatics. We worked together for about 3-4 years and have stayed in touch for the past 30 years.

Mr. Soldinger would always tell the boulder story...picking up the same rock and hoping and praying that the guards didn't know. How frightening that must have been. Also, the electrician's story...trying to fix a light, had no idea what in the world he was doing, but was trying to just find a way to stay alive. Luckily for him as he was getting ready to "try" and fix an electrical problem there was an outage. What in the world? He was saved again.

What I see in Laura is what her dad instilled in her: work hard, be good to others, take advantage of opportunities and make them happen, give back, be honest and don't let fear overrun your life.

Mr. Soldinger was an amazing man for what he went through, how he managed to escape death multiple times, and still believed in good and worked hard for everything he had. His demeanor was good, be kind, be smart, give back to others because you never know what they are going through. That is Laura to a "T" and she has carried on all her father's qualities by being good, caring, compassionate, loving and giving. She is a special person and Sam did an amazing job raising her.

Mr. Soldinger's life could have been much different, but he made the choice to live, be good, work hard, give back and felt blessed with every opportunity that was before him. Laura does the same.

Tana Martin
2021

My grandparents, Ora and Herman "Hap" Laswell eloped when they were teenagers and were married at the beginning of The Great Depression. My grandma's original wedding ring was a simple band with a tiny diamond chip. When their 25th Anniversary arrived, Grandpa Laswell, who was a farmer, walked into the house, pulled a full wedding ring set out of the pocket of his overalls, and said to Grandma Laswell, "better late than never."

Decades later, in the early 1990s, I was visiting Grandma Laswell one weekend at her small home in Cottonwood, Arizona. Grandpa Laswell had passed many years earlier. Grandma suddenly took off the 25th Anniversary wedding set, handed it to me and said that she wanted me to have it. She said that if Tom (my boyfriend at the time) and I decided to get married, I could use it to create my own wedding set if I would like. She then put her original ring on her finger.

Tom and I were engaged a few months later, and we had no idea how to take Grandma's wedding ring set and make it our own. We were very fortunate that our good friend Valerie Lee had a dear friend, Laura Soldinger, whose father was a diamond cutter. That is how Tom and I met Sam Soldinger.

By the time we met him, Sam was semi-retired. He hosted us at his home. He was welcoming, friendly and business-like. He examined the wedding ring set through his eye loupe. We could tell that the diamonds were not of the highest quality, but he understood the priceless sentimental value to us. He told us more than once, as we met and discussed our wedding set, that "it will be beautiful." We discussed options and settled on a design that was similar to the original set. We placed a few small diamonds from the original set into Tom's ring and then added a couple of tiny new diamonds. It felt perfect to us.

When we picked up the wedding set, it was truly beautiful. Tom got down on one knee in front of Sam's house and officially proposed, presenting me with the engagement ring. Grandma Laswell had the pleasure of seeing me wear the wedding set. She loved what Sam had created from her original rings. I was a reporter at the time for Fox 10 Arizona and she enjoyed seeing the ring on television!

In 2021, Tom and I visited the Chandler Museum to see the exhibition about Sam's life. We previously were unaware of all that he had endured and his incredible survival story. After seeing the exhibition, it made our visit with him even more meaningful. We will always treasure our wedding set, and will be forever grateful that we had the fortune to work with such an amazing man to create this beautiful family keepsake.

Julie and Tom Rodriguez
2021

Dear Laura,

Wow, wow, wow. What a life! Sam's story is a testament of his courage, bravery and fortitude.

Robin Stillwell Harvey
2021

We have all read the accounts the Jewish population suffered during the Holocaust of World War II, but it is not until you have actually spoken with a survivor that you truly understand their horrific suffering. In 1993, Mr. Soldinger and his daughter Laura invited my sister and me to attend the premiere of "Schindler's List" in Tucson, Arizona. He shared a great deal during our trip from Phoenix to Tucson, but it wasn't until after viewing the movie that more intimate details were shared. Without any hesitation, he stayed up until the wee hours of the morning talking and answering our questions about his personal ordeal. Those stories have stayed deep within my memories, and even to this day, bring tears to my eyes. Yet, despite what he endured, he was such a happy, positive person. I never saw him without a huge smile and he always greeted you with a hug. I have the deepest respect for Mr. Soldinger and the impact that he had on my life.

Chula Eslamieh
2022

In my first semester of college, my new friend Laura brought me to dinner with her father, Sam. This was my first-time meeting him. Almost 40 years later, I remember we went to his favorite restaurant, Houston's. I don't recall what we ate or every detail of our conversation that night, but I have never forgotten Sam's happiness and kindness. He was so excited and inviting. He loved every second of time with his daughter and welcomed her new friend. In my first-time meeting Sam, I felt like I had known him for years. He was a loving father who embraced life and family. Our happy, carefree conversations never gave a glimpse into what he endured.

It was not until years later with the making of Schindler's List" and his motivational speaking that I learned he was a Holocaust and Schindler survivor. He lost almost all his family and friends. Yet he showed no anger, or at least never showed it in our conversations. It is amazing how a man who endured so much trauma and loss can be so positive, loving, and focused on the present. Every day he embraced his life, his work, his community, and his family. Sam is a testament to the perseverance of the human spirit, which can overcome unspeakable horrors and still emerge optimistic, selfless, compassionate. I am so fortunate to have known and shared time with him.

Sandy Chasnoff Lilienstein
2022

Sam, may he rest in peace.

He was our real friend. We met Sam after one of his speaking engagements at our church in Glendale, Ariz. in 1994. My wife and I both hail from Krakow, Poland. We used to get together every Christmas Eve along with our mutual friends Paul and Leeann Wieser.

Sam mentioned that his mother used to dress the Christmas tree even being Jewish. This is how the Polish and Jewish cultures blended and created special mixture. The Krakow population of Jews was about 20 percent and some of them were not especially religious, celebrating both Christian and Jewish holidays. This goes back centuries.

On our Christmas Eve, we would enjoy traditional Polish dishes like borscht with special tortellini stuffed with mushrooms, fried fish and red cabbage. We also made some Jewish dishes. Sam loved macaroni with poppy seeds blended with honey.

Sam had a phenomenal memory, knowing all his neighbors, small shops nearby and street names back in Krakow. He also talked about his meeting Schindler and how he survived the Holocaust. We really appreciated our meetings.

Tadeusz Swidzinski
2022

Mr. Soldinger was the sweetest – and so handsome!

Sitting in my dental chair, he would relay his lifetime of stories. Where most would be nervous just being at the dentist, he was calm and steady. In between my drilling and fixing has teeth, he would joke, impart wisdom and share stories of his life. I remember his inner strength and love for his fellow human beings. I was mesmerized by his strong, yet gentle, demeanor.

Mr. Soldinger had me listening like never before. We had several appointments just to chat. He taught me how to be more focused when people spoke to me. He taught me about the power of kindness to others. He taught me how to have hope without despair. Bitterness was something he had every right to feel, but Mr. Soldinger held his head high and with that beautiful smile of his, imparted love into my life!

Dr. Margo Rubenstein
2022

Mr. Soldinger had the warmest welcoming eyes, loving spirit and grace. I will never forget the visits we had, the talks we shared.

From my first meeting with him on a trip to Las Vegas with he and Laura, to discussions about jewelry as my grandfather had also been in the industry, to him talking with students that I worked with in Tempe Elementary School District regarding his journey and survival during a tragic time in history, he had such love, warmth and compassion toward others. He always wanted to know "How are you?" and was fully present, engaged and genuinely interested.

Yet with everything his life journey endured, I always wanted to know more about, "How are you Mr. Soldinger?" What wisdom, guidance and insight can you share with me about this crazy thing called life?

With everything he went through as a youngster, his resilience, perseverance and gratitude was never lost. As Mr. Soldinger shared stories of his family, his experiences, his admiration for Mr. Schindler helping him be the sole survivor of his family, he always spoke with such warmth, commitment and compassion to others. Mr. Soldinger, despite what he went through, did not have hate nor understand it. He understood love. Compassion. Education to others to help those ahead of us never endure nor experience nor be a part of the trauma and hurt and harm he endured.

Mr. Soldinger leaves behind a beautiful family and legacy within his daughter, Laura, to carry forward his values, beliefs and unconditional love for others. I will forever keep in my heart our times together, conversations shared, bread we broke with a simple meal together; the sharing with children of his journey to adulthood to help them be mindful of how to love and not hate others, and his overall essence of being true to himself and ability to rise up to greatness.

We love you Sam. We miss you Sam. You shared your story with grace, helping inspire and educate others. I am grateful to you and in admiration of who you were, and you continue to be in spirit watching over your friends and family.

Wendy Collison
2022

Even though Sam rarely called me by the correct name - to him I was Cindy, not Wendi - I will never forget him. As a child, I was fascinated by the fact that he spoke so many languages and I loved hearing him speak. I have fond memories of sitting, captivated, listening to the stories and recollections of his Holocaust experience. I was incredulous at times, wondering how anyone could go through what he went through and come out seemingly unscathed. Often full of unsolicited advice, Sam Soldinger was a generous, intelligent and incredibly interesting man and I'm thankful to have known him.

Wendi Hunter Pinchen
2022

With a heart full of love
Never without a smile
Always positive
Caring
Honest
Inspiring

I can see precious Sam smiling from heaven. He would be humbled, honored and proud that his life will continue blessing and inspiring others.

Thanking God he crossed our path—with the added gift of becoming friends with his beautiful daughter, Laura.

Danny & Idamarie Marchetti
Etruscan Gold Ltd.
Custom Design Jeweler
Phoenix, Arizona
(Business from 1971 - 2011)
2022

Life-changing memories of time spent with Samuel Soldinger:

A front-page article in the *Arizona Republic* about the newly released movie "Schindler's List" caught my attention. It was already a mesmerizing story, but the minute I saw the name Samuel Soldinger and that he had a daughter in Phoenix, I was hooked on finding out more about this amazing man and survivor!

I picked up the phone and called the Special Events Office for the City of Phoenix. I asked to speak to Laura Soldinger and was told she was not there. Since I knew the people in the office, I implored them to tell me if it was Laura's father who was the Holocaust survivor. The person on the other end of the phone asked who was asking and I gave her my name, which of course she recognized. "Hang on a minute" was the reply. Less than a minute later, Laura was on the line explaining that she was in the office but was getting ready to go to Tucson for a preview showing of "Schindler's List" with her father. I begged her to set up a time that I could meet him and thus started a relationship with Mr. Soldinger that has already spanned three generations of my family and will continue to live on in the stories we tell.

I am so grateful to Laura for being gracious in arranging multiple meetings with her father. Each meeting was distinctive, but the greetings were always the same. Mr. Soldinger would welcome with a warm smile, embrace with a light kiss on each cheek and a firm grip of the hand. He would insist that I could call him by Sam, but I could never bring myself to do it. He was always "Mr. Soldinger."

Personally, I thought I had listened closely in those meetings with Mr. Soldinger. I took pride in bringing a notebook and jotting down key points of the conversation. Boy, did I find out I was wrong! I will never forget being seated in an upscale restaurant on 24th Street and Camelback in Phoenix when I received the lesson of a lifetime! The booth had tall backs for privacy between diners and the table was set with china plates, crystal goblets and linen tablecloths. I was always hooked on every word of his stories but because of his heavy accent, I had to listen closely to what he was saying to make sure I did not miss anything. Not this time! We had already finished dinner, but the dishes were still on the table. Mr. Soldinger was telling in more detail about the atrocities he witnessed and those inflicted on him. Without thinking, I blurted out that I did not understand why he was not angry and hateful of certain groups of people for what they had done to him and for everything he had endured. I was on a roll and did not give him time to get a word in! I said that I could not understand how Laura had grown up and become one of the kindest individuals I knew and how she would always find the good in people. I had seen this trait in Laura long before I met Mr. Soldinger, but knowing her father's history now made it unbelievable to me that they could be so loving, acceptable, and kind!

And, then came the thunder! Or so it seemed! As his open hand hit the table, the crystal goblets shook and the china plates danced, as he exclaimed "You haven't listened!" At the time, I was sure the entire restaurant heard his booming voice, but in retrospect I am sure it was because the words were reverberating in my head.

Then he shared his lesson in life in the simplest of terms. It is not about nationality. It is about the individual person. It is about expecting the best from everyone. There are good people everywhere and more good people in the world than bad. He went on to say that he only survived because of the extra food he was given, or shoes provided by guards so he could work; individuals who would have suffered dire consequences had they been caught. He gave example after example of how his life was saved by ordinary people, and of course, those examples included Oskar Schindler. We went on to have other meaningful meetings, but his wise words changed my life.

Once a year, the administrators and producers of life and health insurance companies would come together for a luncheon with a featured guest speaker. The guest speakers were usually ho-hum, and the luncheons were not usually well attended. I was on the luncheon planning committee and mentioned that I could arrange for Mr. Soldinger to be the speaker. With that, the event exploded! There had never been so many reservations. We had to change the venue three times because people kept responding! We finally had to stop accepting reservations because we could not find another location to move it to. Mr. Soldinger did not disappoint. Some of the most successful businesspeople of Phoenix were there and were unashamedly moved to tears. The standing ovation lasted for several minutes.

Years later, people who were there would recount his story and I have no doubt that they have shared it, just as I have, with friends, family, and their next generation. Mr. Soldinger only had one request: that I tell the story so that the story and history would be kept alive. I promised him that I would, and I have kept that promise. My grandchildren know all about Mr. Sam Soldinger. They have heard his stories. They have watched "Schindler's List." They too, will carry on his story.

My children, who were teenagers when they met Mr. Soldinger, were so impacted by his story that we were inspired to visit the New York and Washington D.C. Holocaust museums. We traveled to Germany and visited the Dachau Concentration Camp Memorial. Over the years, we have continued to read and study about the Holocaust to obtain even more knowledge so that we can accurately share even more stories. Mr. Sam Soldinger lives on in all of us!

Ima Jean Dolan
Phoenix Community Volunteer
2022

A DAUGHTER'S REFLECTIONS

Laura and Sam in Las Vegas.

Growing up as a daughter of a Holocaust survivor has been beyond enlightening and hard to even fathom what my father Samuel Soldinger - and others like him - endured. He was such a sweet man, and at first glance or by a casual, neighborly conversation, one would never know all he had been through.

My father raised us to always have a positive outlook on life, and never harbor hate or be prejudiced toward anyone. He always spoke positively in difficult situations. He enriched all of our lives and we are better because of it.

My earliest memory getting a glimpse into my father's horrific background was when I was 4 years old, asking him to tell me a story of when he was a child. He replied that I would have to wait to hear these stories when I was older, as the stories would give me nightmares. I always said that he could tell me, I wouldn't get nightmares . . . little did I know the atrocities that he overcame to survive.

As I entered my teens, he began sharing his stories with me and always wanted me to write "his book." He would have me watch every movie or documentary that came out about the Holocaust. My father was rare as he always wanted to share his story, while most of his friends didn't want to talk or remember the horrors that they had endured. He started working on his memoirs many years before he died. He did interviews and speaking engagements on the Holocaust on occasion, but it wasn't until the 1994 release of "Schindler's List" that my father truly was able to get his story out. He was in high demand and everyone wanted to hear about his experiences and learn of the atrocities that occurred firsthand. Steven Spielberg became a personal savior of my father's and also of mine. My father wanted his story told to share the lessons of a painful journey and hopefully be a source of inspiration for peace for generations to come.

While we had the treasures of his handwriting in bold strokes from a Sharpie on large yellow notepads and tapes of interviews he'd given, now his story had lied dormant again in the years since "Schindler's List" in a simple cardboard box of scrapbook clippings in my closet. It was a yearning and passion of his, and of mine, that his story become a book and join those who have recounted their unimaginable experiences of the Holocaust with the years of healing that followed.   But how?   I'll admit, the thought was overwhelming to put it together to properly give him, and those alongside him, the justice of their voices heard and their harrowing experiences remembered. It wasn't until a series of chance meetings did the light bulb go on for me.

In 2007, I took a new position within the City of Phoenix, marketing golf courses. My new boss mentioned that she grew up in Chandler, Ariz., so I asked her if she had ever heard of the Harry Winston diamond factory. She hadn't but said that she would ask her older brother and mentioned that he still lived in Chandler and was involved with the Chandler community. Fast forward to the summer of 2018. I am now retired and spending the summer in San Diego. I received a phone call from my former boss's brother, Tom Escobedo, who is on the board of the Chandler Museum and he asked if I have any photos or memorabilia from the Harry Winston diamond factory that my father managed in the 1960s, '70s and '80s.

I of course do, so he arranged a meeting with the museum. When I met with staff and donated pictures and memorabilia, I also shared a few articles showcasing my father's experiences with the Holocaust. They were very excited, as the museum had only one photo of the diamond plant from when it was first built in 1962. That was it.

Not thinking much more about it, a year later, in the summer of 2019, I received a call from the Chandler Museum Curator of Collections at the time, Nate Meyers, telling me that my father's story was added to their speaker series for February 2020 and asked if I would be interested in sharing his story. I was so excited to hear this news! Having a fear of public speaking, I politely declined and asked Nate if he would be willing to speak on my behalf, and I would be there to answer questions. He graciously accepted. On February 29, 2020, I attended the presentation with my family and was absolutely blown away! The presentation was so well attended that chairs had to be added outside of the large auditorium. Nate must have researched and worked on the presentation for months on end! He did such an amazing job of sharing my dad's story that I had an epiphany: this is the book!

The COVID-19 pandemic hit shortly after the presentation and a close friend of mine, Valerie Lee, who is a brilliant writer, was laid off work. I had another epiphany and approached her about taking on this project. Valerie agreed and thus this book project was launched. From the box of my father's notes, video presentations, newspaper articles and past book efforts, Valerie wove the details into a beautiful tapestry from Sam's own storytelling. I know that my father is looking down on us from heaven and is absolutely elated – his dream of the book is finally fulfilled!

In writing the book amid the coronavirus pandemic of 2020, I was also looking at the incomparable, uneven parallels of then and now. This is the first time in my lifetime that I have experienced anything like this. People are quarantined to their homes, most businesses are closed, people are out of work, the economy is suffering, and businesses are stepping up to make masks for the good of the cause. Takes me back to Schindler's factory and making ammunition for the war effort. I think about those who were in hiding in confined spaces for years. We are being asked to self-quarantine in our homes with electronics, television, Wi-Fi, gorgeous backyards . . . and it is so "tough" to not live our "normal" lives and go and come as we please. It is so petty compared to what others have gone through and endured. We are so fortunate to live in the United States with so many freedoms and opportunities. We live such great lives and have everything we could ever ask for or need. This is a good reminder that the small sacrifices that we make will hopefully save many lives and rid the virus so people can get back to normal. Now in 2021, it is much brighter with vaccines, and the virus waning, the economy is coming back and hopefully many positive things will come out of this.

When my father first showed me the book, "Schindler's List," he talked about how most of the "characters" were his friends or acquaintances. My dad never forgot a face and remembered everyone he ever met. His friends were his family and he kept in close contact with those he met during the Holocaust and in the displaced persons camps after the war.

My father often spoke about Ben Friedman, his electrician friend. Ben immigrated to Israel after the war. I met Ben in Israel in 1981, when I traveled there with my stepbrother Zachary. He was very short in stature and drove a Volkswagen Beetle. He picked us up from the airport in Tel Aviv and got the two of us settled into a hostel, as we were traveling alone. He was very kind and couldn't do enough to help us. On that trip, we also stayed with my dad's friend Louis Oppenheim (also mentioned in this book) and his family. It was wonderful to meet two of my dad's lifelong friends, as they had all gone through the horrors of the Holocaust together.

As my father shared the stories of his life and the people he cherished, not only did he credit Oskar Schindler for saving his life, but he also credited Dr. Samuel Rubinstein. After the war, Dr. Rubinstein changed his name to Stanley Robbin. My father and Dr. Robbin reconnected after liberation and corresponded throughout their lives. In 2023, while in the process of editing this book, I connected with Dr. Robbin's son Mark and his wife Lois Robbin through Facebook. I learned that their grandson Dylan Robbin is working on his bar mitzvah project related to the Holocaust. While reading about his grandfather's Holocaust experiences, Dylan learned that his grandfather saved a young man named Samuel Soldinger. I recently had the honor of meeting Mark and Lois Robbin and their beloved grandson Dylan. We have all become fast friends.

My dad definitely knew and understood people. He always used to say that he was not the smartest guy, but he understood people and had common sense. He definitely learned early, as he had to use this gift many times throughout his years in concentration camps. He also taught me how making good friends and keeping them would enrich my life. He used to say that if you had a handful of close friends you were blessed. He was such a good friend and always kept in touch with people. Most of his friends from Europe were scattered all over the world, but he always maintained a good friendship with them by being in constant contact with them and visiting when he could. He was a firm believer about choosing good friends who would positively influence my life. I definitely think that I have done a good job with choosing my friends.

My father's good friend, Henri Landwirth, a Holocaust survivor and founder of Give Kids the World, was close friends with John Glenn and the Mercury 7 astronauts and presented my father with a signed photo of the astronauts in front of a USAF F106. My dad cherished this photo as it represented freedom and the American dream. It always hung in his office since the 1960s. When I met my husband Matt in 2010, he had served nearly three decades in the U.S. Air Force, and I knew my dad would have been so proud to have him as a son-in-law. Matt retired as a colonel, which is prestigious as only a very small percentage of officers in the USAF earn this rank. Another thing my dad would have admired.

My father was so proud to be an American and told me often how lucky I was to be born in America. He used to say that there is nothing like the United States. I did not fully appreciate or understand his love for America until I traveled to Israel my senior year of high school in 1981. Everywhere we traveled, we would see Israeli military carrying machine guns. They were everywhere. You would think this would have made me feel safe, but it seemed to just make me aware that there was a constant threat. We were never safe. When traveling on a public bus, there was a random stop and police came on board and made each of us claim our baggage to ensure no one had left a bomb on board. I also saw a bicycle confiscated because no one would claim it and it could have been hiding a bomb. It was surreal, crazy and nothing I had ever experienced. The Wailing Wall in Jerusalem was surrounded by police and military protecting the sacred area.

Once I returned home, I remember thinking, "I love America!" It made me realize the freedoms we have.

When 9/11 happened nine months after my father died in 2001, I remember thinking how glad I was that he did not live to see this happen to his America. Those things never happen here. That hate belongs somewhere else, and by that I mean, hate doesn't belong anywhere at all.

I am the youngest child of Samuel. I was born in 1964 in Phoenix. My brothers David Jacob (October 22, 1954-November 21, 2020) and Adam Bruce (October 28, 1957-February 16, 2021) were both born in Brooklyn, N.Y. My dad married my mother, Saralee Salzberg (March 12, 1928 – August 20, 2003) in New York on March 1, 1951, after he immigrated to New York City on July 8, 1950.

My father met my mother at a dance. He looked across the room and saw my mother, who was stunningly beautiful, and told his friend, Curt Storch, that he was going to marry her! Curt is still alive today, living in New York, and he shares that story with me every time I see him.

One time, my parents were walking in Manhattan and a famous movie star happened to pass them on the street; the movie star turned as he passed my mom to admire her. My dad shared this story with me many times. My father had fallen in love with my mother immediately, as well as her parents and brother. He felt very comfortable at my mother's parents' house. My grandfather was from Poland and my grandmother would make home cooked meals for my dad almost nightly. My father and my mother married just six weeks later.

My father was cutting diamonds in the Diamond District in New York City and my parents bought a home in Flatbush (Brooklyn) on Avenue J, which was a predominately Jewish neighborhood. They were raising my two brothers and spent a lot of time with family. My grandmother had two sisters in Brooklyn and all of their extended families were there. They spent summers in the Catskills and enjoyed a very nice life.

When my dad accepted the position with Harry Winston and moved the family to Phoenix, my mom had a tough time. The Jewish community in Phoenix was very small in the early '60s, so it was a bit of an adjustment for her compared to back East, plus learning to drive and making new friends. My mom also suffered from depression, which began in her teens. My dad was busy running the factory and my mom seemed to have problems coping. She loved to knit and embroider, play cards, mahjong and bingo.

Sam in front of his first home in Phoenix.

My parents were married for 20 years. I was 6 years old when they separated and 10 when they finally divorced. Both of my parents remarried, and both ultimately divorced. My dad remarried in 1978 to Geraldine, who had three children from a previous marriage: Selina, Zachary and Brian. They were all around my age, which was great fun for me, being a part of a larger family. My stepmom worked for the airlines so she and my dad traveled the world! We also took family vacations, went on annual ski trips and took several trips to Disneyland. My dad and Geri bought a beautiful home together in Northeast Phoenix. Geri took a job transfer initially to Los Angeles and then Minneapolis. They would travel back and forth, but eventually it wasn't working. They remained good friends and would see each other for dinner when Geri was in town. She was 16 years younger than my dad and loved to travel. With my dad's heart condition, travel eventually became difficult for him and he enjoyed being at home and loved the Arizona climate.

My brothers, being 7 and 10 years older than I am, both experienced a lot of anti-Semitism as young boys in Phoenix, which at the time as I mentioned had a very small Jewish population. They both played ice hockey and I remember hearing stories of them being called names or picked on because of their religion. I mention this because it made a very big impression on me as a young girl. I rarely would tell friends that I was Jewish for fear of being picked on. I still run into friends from high school who learn of my father's story and they tell me that they had no idea that I was Jewish. I never wore a Jewish Star or symbol. This was the reason why.

My dad spoke seven languages and when I brought friends home, he would always ask their last name and tell them what their name meant in German, Polish, etc. My best friend in 6th grade was Stacy Gossard. I don't remember what her name meant, but I knew it was a German name. I remember wondering, should I be hanging around someone who is German? I quickly learned through my father that there are good people and bad people throughout every walk of life – do not judge someone by their ethnicity, religion, or any other factor except the character of their heart. This is one of the things I admired most about my father: his ability to always see the good in people.

One of my father's favorite places was Las Vegas. We would vacation there three or four times a year. We always stayed at the Dunes Hotel. It was very opulent in the '60s and '70s and it had a great nursery for me. The nursery had beds and my parents would gamble into the night and then carry me from the nursery up to our hotel room. My dad quickly befriended the staff. I still have fond memories of Polly, who was my favorite. I also got to meet Cary Grant in the Dunes Nursery. I played with his daughter Jennifer and helped her make a necklace. He came over and thanked me and they had paged my mom to come meet him as well. He was one of her favorite actors and she was thrilled!

Cousins Sam and Harry Soldinger.

In the summer of 1976, I was away at summer camp. My dad was in Las Vegas playing blackjack at the Dunes Hotel when he heard a page (pick up a white paging phone) for Soldinger. He answered the page and heard a young girl's voice. Of course, he thought that it was me and said in his heavy Polish accent, "Laura?" He hears, "No, this is Carol and you're not my dad." My dad asked her if she paged Sam Soldinger, she said, "No, I paged my father, Harry Soldinger." On the phone standing next to my dad was Harry Soldinger. It turns out they were cousins and became lifelong friends. After this meeting, we always saw Harry and his beautiful wife Rene on every trip to Vegas.

Soldinger Family Crest

Harry and his family were the first cousins I met who had the Soldinger name. My father, being the only survivor of his immediate family, initially reached out to extended family when he arrived in New York. He was not well received unfortunately, so he stopped reaching out. My mom had a younger brother, Herman Salzberg and his wife Adele. We were very close to them, but we really did not have many close relative relationships.

222

In 1981, Florence Soldinger Zisman and her husband Stanley retired to Scottsdale, Ariz. While looking up Smitty's grocery store in the local phone book, she saw SOLDINGER at the top of the page and then looked at the list of Soldingers: David and Samuel. Surprised, shocked and amazed, she closed the phone book. The reason she was stunned is that her father's name was Samuel Soldinger and he had died when she was 17. She finally got the courage to call my father and they became fast friends. Another cousin/friend! Florence was also like a mother to me. She and Stanley were amazing golfers and always encouraged me to golf. Florence had me over for weekly meals and lox and bagels on Sunday mornings, which was wonderful. Florence passed away at the age of 97 in 2015. She certainly lived life to the fullest, was vivacious and was the life of the party! She too is missed very much.

My dad met other cousins coincidentally . . . while picking up a prescription in Phoenix, the pharmacist said that his mother-in-law's maiden name is Soldinger. This connects us to a family of eight Soldingers that hail from Toledo, Ohio.

In 1989, Harry Soldinger hosted a Soldinger Family Reunion in Las Vegas at the Riviera Hotel. Between Harry, Florence, my dad and the Toledo cousins, over 100 cousins attended! Cousin Ruben Soldinger and some of his brothers from the Toledo contingency put together a Family Tree and Crest and we all of the sudden were a large family! I met and became close to Geri Katzman Welsh (Lannie and Roanne Soldinger Katzman's daughter) and became very close with her parents who visited often and became my parents once mine had both passed.

Harry Soldinger's daughter Carol and I have become close in the last several years and my husband Matt and I see her and her husband Dave Levins several times a year. Carol's seventh grandson is named Harry Winston Hall, born to her son Jared Hall and his wife Dasha. How perfect to now have a Harry Winston in the family!

As mentioned earlier, my father was born on August 28, 1924, and 28 was always his lucky number. In my lifetime and especially since my dad passed away, the number 28 and 828 seems to play a significant role in my life. My husband Matt Yotter and I coincidentally married on August 28, 2011, after narrowing down a date when all of his children and my nephew could attend.

Another example is the first time I visited Krakow, Poland in 2007, when I rented a flat. When I arrived at the condominium complex and schlepped my heavy bags up a gazillion flights of stairs to a lovely Polish girl waving to us out the window of the unit, we arrived at the door to unit #28! On that same trip, my friend Trish and I had taken a weeklong bus tour and when we arrived in Prague, the tour guide began calling out names and giving us our room keys. I thought for sure we would get room 28, but no, we got room number 4. As we were unpacking our bags, there was a knock at our door. One of the girls on the tour was traveling with her brother and had been given a room with a king size bed and was hoping we would switch with them as we had two single beds. We of course agreed and low and behold, we switched to room #28! I retired from the City of Phoenix after 28 years of full-time service! My husband Matt served our country in the U.S. Air Force for 28 years! Every time I see number 28 or 8:28 on a clock, I think of my father and feel that this is one of many signs that he is watching over me.

My father would tell me how growing up in Krakow, they were poor. He said if he and his friends found a nickel, the other kids would run to the candy store and my father would run to the corner market for a piece of cheese. He loved cheese. When we were growing up in Phoenix, we always had imported cheese in the house. His favorite butcher was "Cheese 'n Stuff" in central Phoenix, which was run by a local German family, and they would always let us sample the cheese as they sliced the cheese and wrapped the packages.

My father loved sports. He told me about going to watch soccer with his father in Krakow. He also learned how to snow ski as a kid. He and his friends would carry their skis up a nearby mountain and ski down. He also played soccer, as a goalie, and was proud to show me that he could defend the ball with his head! After the war, he took up ping-pong and was a ping-pong champion in Europe. He continued playing in America and I still have several of his ping-pong trophies that I cherish. Growing up, we always had a ping-pong table and there were ping-pong tables at the Harry Winston diamond factory in Chandler, Ariz., for the employees to play at lunchtime and during their breaks, where my father was a manager for nearly 20 years.

As you can imagine, the Harry Winston diamond factory was very highly secured. Off duty Chandler Police were on site whenever the factory was open. The diamonds that were cut at the factory were small industrial diamonds averaging .10 carats. The Native Americans would check out a parcel of diamonds to cut. They were counted out and in. Before they were passed on to the next area for cutting, each diamond had to be examined by either my father, or the foreman, Boris Iwanier. My dad would open each parcel, pour out the diamonds and inspect each one, separating the bad from the good. He would then put them back into their parcel paper to either go to the next station or back to be recut. At the close of each day, all of the diamonds were securely packed by diamond parcel into a large case and my dad was police-escorted to Valley National Bank in Chandler where the diamonds were stored in the vault. The VNB vault is now a part of San Tan Brewery in Downtown Chandler.

Chandler was a very small town in the 1960s, and although we always lived in Phoenix, Chandler felt like home. My dad was very involved with the Chamber of Commerce and at one point was President of the Chamber of Commerce. He was also very involved with the Bureau of Indian Affairs (BIA) and often attended Tribal meetings. He was always doing what he could for the Native Americans. I remember dressing up for Halloween and passing out candy at the factory. Every employee received a turkey or a ham to take home at Thanksgiving and Christmas.

At Christmastime, my dad would buy cases of liquor and See's chocolates to give as gifts to friends and business acquaintances. He was always so kind and giving. He would take things to his doctor's office, friends, neighbors and places he frequented. He was friendly and kind to everyone and was always quick to make friends.

As an executive with Harry Winston, he was given a company car every three years. I remember him having an LTD when I was little, but he almost exclusively drove an Oldsmobile after that. He also earned generous bonuses each year. He wore a suit and tie most days to work. He loved clothes and was always well dressed. He would buy beautiful suits and have them tailored to fit and bought beautiful silk ties. We spent a lot of time at Park Central Mall in central Phoenix. His two favorite department stores were Diamond's and Goldwater's. Another executive perk of working for Harry Winston was that he could buy season tickets to one of the local sports teams. We had four seats to the Phoenix Roadrunners hockey team and would attend games at Phoenix Veterans Memorial Coliseum. I have many fond memories of attending hockey games with my dad.

My dad also treated us to other landmark Phoenix favorites such as the old-fashioned Mary Coyle's ice cream parlor and family dinners at Durant's steakhouse. At Durant's, I always ordered a Shirley Temple and a salad with Roquefort dressing. We always had the same waiter, Tommy.

When the Harry Winston diamond factory closed due to the economy in 1982, my dad chose to take an early retirement. While he had the opportunity to stay with Harry Winston, it would have meant moving back to New York or China.

After my father retired from Harry Winston, he started selling diamonds and jewelry out of our home. He never advertised but ran the small business on word of mouth. He had such a great reputation as a diamond expert and everyone trusted him. He always tried to educate people on diamonds before selling to them, so that they knew and understood what they were buying. He never went anywhere without a loupe and would always check people's rings to make sure that the prongs around their diamonds were tight. After college, when my friends started getting engaged, I kept my dad busy selling engagement rings. So many of my friends still have their rings and fondly show off their ring from Sam! My dad was always telling me that he could always tell a lot about a person when it came to picking out an engagement ring. He thought it was most proper to be happy with a stone/ring that the gentleman could afford. The ladies that would "demand" a bigger or better stone above what their fiancé could afford was not right. He would always tell me that I should be happy with what I was given. I could always upgrade when times and monies were better.

During his retirement years in Phoenix, he spent a lot of time at Café Casino at 24th Street and Camelback Road near the Cine Capri movie theater. He would go there daily for coffee and kibbitz with people. He loved meeting new people. When Café Casino closed, he moved across the street to Coffee Plantation and would spend most of his mornings there. My friends and colleagues would often run into him and would always enjoy chatting with him. He also used to frequent Houston's and would sit at the bar, have dinner, and talk to the bartender and guests. He rarely drank alcohol, but just enjoyed being with people and sharing stories. Oscar Taylor was also one of his favorite restaurants at Biltmore Fashion Park and he loved shopping at The Broadway at Biltmore Fashion Park. He bought so many pairs of shoes there that he became good friends with the shoe salesman. The Biltmore shopping district was fairly close to his house and he spent a lot of time in the area.

My oldest brother David married in 1985. He and his wife Suncha Choung had one son, Paul Bernard Soldinger on October 25, 1985. They divorced in 1999 and both stayed active in Paul's life. Paul graduated from the University at Arizona earning a bachelor's degree in Accounting, and currently is a CPA for the State of Arizona. Paul married Sandi Thoi in 2012 and they have two beautiful children, Cora Skye Soldinger (2016) and Zayla Celeste Soldinger (2019), and they reside in Mesa, Ariz.

My dad passed away on January 2, 2001, of heart failure. During his time in the camps, he contracted rheumatic fever that weakened his heart valves and he battled the repercussions of that throughout the rest of his life, which included two open-heart surgeries in his later years. He had fractured his back in September of 2000 and had become somewhat bedridden. Mentally, he was very sharp, but he was in a lot of pain and it became difficult for him to get out of bed.

In Judaism, it is customary to bury the dead within 24-48 hours. He was laid to rest on January 4, 2001. Oddly enough, it was one of the most special days of my life. My stepsister's husband, Rabbi Michael Rovinsky, flew in from St. Louis, Mo., to conduct the service. He gave the most beautiful eulogy. Mount Sinai Mortuary in Phoenix, where the service was held, was filled to capacity. There was such an outpouring of love. I was very touched by this. He was buried in shroud as in Judaism it is believed that you come into this world with nothing and you leave this world with nothing in a simple casket (another Jewish tradition). He is buried at Paradise Memorial Gardens in Scottsdale, Ariz.

Although it was winter in Arizona, January 4, 2001, was a beautiful 70-degree day. When I arrived at my home following the burial, I noticed that there was a beautiful yellow butterfly flying around the yard. Being January, I was surprised to see a butterfly, but it was very comforting. Ever since then, yellow butterflies always remind me of my dad. When my mother passed away in August 2003 after suffering with Alzheimer's disease for seven years, when I returned home from her burial, there were two yellow butterflies in the yard!

I seem to have constant reminders of my amazing father. I feel that he is always with me and watching over me. I think of him often and especially love when I dream of him. It's as if we are still together.

In 2003, a cousin who I barely knew, Vicki Aguilar-Case was in town with her mother, Janice Soldinger for the Fiesta Bowl. Her brother, Don Soldinger, coached for The Miami Hurricanes. Vicki's father, Howard Soldinger, had also passed away and she was telling me that she had gone to see a world-renowned medium to see if her father would come through. She then proceeded to tell me that my father had come through and he was with his mother Adele. He wanted her to tell me that he wants his book written! I had to laugh as now my dad was haunting me from his grave about his book! If he were to come through during someone's psychic reading, that is exactly the message that he would send to me!

In 2015, my husband and I traveled to Europe and were able to visit several concentration camps that are now museums. The first camp we toured was Dachau just outside of Munich, Germany. Dachau was the first concentration camp built by Nazi Germany in March 1933. It was originally used for Hitler's political opponents that consisted of communists, social democrats and other dissidents. Eventually it imprisoned Jews, Gypsies, German and

Austrian criminals. My father was in Dachau for only a short time.

The second camp we visited was Auschwitz I and Auschwitz II - Birkenau in Oswiecim, Poland. We drove from Krakow, Poland, which is about an hour drive. The Auschwitz I tour was very interesting with disturbing artifacts including hair, shoes, suitcases and personal belongings from prisoners.

We then took a short bus ride to Auschwitz II – Birkenau which was a concentration camp and extermination camp with gas chambers. The magnitude of Auschwitz II – Birkenau can only be imagined by physically visiting the camp. Pictures do not fully showcase how immense this killing-field was. Of the 960,000 Jews who were killed there, 865,000 were gassed upon arrival. Luckily, my father only traveled by train through Auschwitz, but never was imprisoned there.

While in Krakow, we also visited Schindler's Factory. The factory has been converted into a very nice museum.

The last camp we visited was Mauthausen in Linz, Austria. We drove from Vienna, Austria and were heading to Salzburg to continue our travels. After driving a few hours, we arrived in Mauthausen, which looked like a beautiful fortress from afar. We were limited on time so were just going to go through the museum and not do a full tour of the grounds. We asked the clerk what she recommended and she said that an English tour had just started and we should join that group. As we were paying, Matt said, "Isn't it moving to be at the camp where your father was liberated?" The clerk overheard Matt and pushed our money back toward us and said, "Your father was here? You don't pay." This immediately brought tears to my eyes. It was such a nice gesture and made me realize the magnitude of what I was about to see.

We joined the tour which included three Jewish students from England who had just graduated from high school and two girls that were college-age from Spain. When we arrived at the top of the rock quarry, I was compelled to share my dad's near-death experience in the quarry. From that point on, the students on the tour had endless questions and wanted to know more. After finishing the tour, we sat with the five tour students for another hour to answer all of their questions and share my father's experiences. The Jewish students also shared their experiences with anti-Semitism in England. It was so refreshing to meet this group of young people who had a thirst to learn about the atrocities that occurred during WWII.

I share this with you to say I am so sorry for all my father went through, for what so many went through, and I am so glad and grateful he survived.

His goodness and character are like ripples in the lake, against a beautiful sunset, and the gentle tides bring all of his lessons, faith and goodwill back to shore. He taught me such high values and to love unconditionally. He was the love of my life and I will carry his teachings, nurturing and spirit with me always.

My father wanted to share his story so "we never forget." From this, I hope that readers have a better understanding of hate, hope and perseverance and I hope that you will share it with your friends, family, children and grandchildren and encourage them to share it as well, lest we never forget.

Laura Soldinger Yotter

Adam, Laura and David Soldinger at Sam's north Phoenix home.

David, Laura and Adam Soldinger in front of Oscar Tylor's restaurant at Biltmore Fashion Park.

232

From left to right (seated): David, Adam and Saralee (standing) Paul, cousins Lisa Smith and Alan Salzberg, Laura and Sam.

From left to right (seated) David, Adam, Saralee (standing) Suncha, Laura, Paul and Sam.

Sam's ping-pong trophies.

Sam celebrating his 75 birthday.

Sam with his beloved grandson Paul.

Laura with her husband Matt Yotter.

From left to right: Saralee, Adam, Laura, and Sam.

"Every survivor has a story. Those who did not survive couldn't tell their story. I can't speak for all these people. I wish I could."

Samuel Soldinger

ACKNOWLEDGEMENTS

Special thanks and grateful appreciation to Nate Meyers, former Curator of Collections at the Chandler Museum in Arizona whose passion for Sam's story, presentations and museum exhibit further propelled our purpose to honor my father's wish of writing this book. To my dear friend Valerie Lee for taking on this project and for piecing it together into a beautiful tapestry and meaningful story. To Nancy Soldinger Embree and David Embree for your beautiful prose and the work you did to document Sam's story. To Lannie Katzman for creating the Soldinger Report Newsletters and helping to unite so many Soldinger cousins. Lannie also has kept Sam's story alive by converting his visual stories to DVDs (VHS-DVD) and endless hours of editing this book. To the USC Shoah Foundation – The Institute for Visual History and Education who documented video interviews. To Max McQueen formerly of *Tribune Newspapers* in Mesa, Arizona for interviewing Sam and sharing his meaningful stories. To my husband, Matt Yotter, for historical fact checking and editing. To my dear friend Jenny Osterland for translating English to German. To all of you, your dedication to this project has helped Sam's dream come true of having his story told for the world to hear. From the bottom of my heart, I thank you.

Laura Soldinger Yotter

REFERENCES

<u>Newspaper and Periodical Articles</u>

Adams, Anita. (Undated). Child of War, Nevermore. *Impact Parenting*, 4.

Ancient Indian Crafts Ability Creating Diamonds. (1965, September 2). *Arizona Daily Sun*, 12.

Diamond Cutting Comes To Arizona. (1965, January 18). *Arizona Daily Star*, B12.

Jensen, Edythe. (2008, April 4). Chandler Landed a Gem of a Business in 1960s. *Arizona Republic/Chandler Republic*, 8.

Kuehlthau, Margaret. (1965, June 5). All That Glitters. *Tucson Citizen*, 18.

Mahoney, Ralph. (1964, May 10). Indians Cut Diamonds At Chandler Plant: Smocked reservation natives hunch over scientific machines to prepare stones for milady's adornment. *Arizona Days and Ways*, 7-10.

McQueen, Max. (1994, January 2). Exclusive Interviews with Schindler's Survivors. *East Valley Tribune*, A1.

McQueen, Max. (1994, January 23). Horrors of the Holocaust. East Valley Tribune, I1.

McQueen, Max. (2001, February 4). Schindler's List survivor lives on in many hearts. *East Valley Tribune*, F1.

Protector in the darkness: List saved some from death camps. (1994, January 10). *Tucson Citizen*, 1B, 3B.

Protector in the darkness: Schindler showed kindness, survivor says. (1994, January 10). *Tucson Citizen*, 1B, 3B.

Samuel Soldinger. (2001, January 4). *Arizona Republic*, B9.
Skinner, M. Scot. (1994, January 9). L.M.I snags grand prize in Rock Wars; 'Schindler's List' to get benefit screening. *Arizona Daily Star*, D4.

Sowers, Carol. (1994, January 12). More Than a Movie: Schindler's list saved Valley pair's lives. *Arizona Republic*, A1, A7.

Taylor, Vince. (1971, November 3). Chandler: Profile of a happily growing community. *Arizona Republic*, 16.

Thomason, Art. (1991, March 30). Death Camp Survivors Reunite. *Arizona Republic*, A1.

Yearwood, Paula. (1994, July 15). Schindler Jew: Film Helps Survivor to Break His Silence. *Jewish News of Greater Phoenix*, 1.

Websites

Harry Winston (2021, November 10) www.harrywinston.com

The Central Database of Shoah Victims' Names: Soldinger, Samuel. In *YadVashem Archives*. https://yvng.yadvashem.org/nameDetails.html?language=en&itemId=4145933&ind=1

Timeline of Events. (2022, March 17). In *United States Holocaust Memorial Museum*. https://www.ushmm.org/learn/timeline-of-events/before-1933

Volksdeutsche. (2022, Sept. 25). In *Shoah Resource Center of YadVashem.org*.

Books

Brecher, Elinor J., ed. *Schindler's Legacy: True Stories of the List Survivors*. Penguin Books, New York, 1994.

Keneally, Thomas. *Schindler's List*. Simon & Schuster, New York, 1994.

Offen, Bernard and Norman G. Jones. *My Hometown Concentration Camp: A Survivor's Account of Life in the Krakow Ghetto and Plaszow Concentration Camp*. Valentine Mitchell, London, England, 2008.

Pankiewicz, Tadeusz. *The Krakow Ghetto Pharmacy*. Wydawnictwo Literackie, Krakow, Poland, 2013. Translated by Wydawnictwo Literackie, 2013.

Pemper, Mietek, Viktoria Hertling, and Marie Elisabeth Muller. *The Road to Rescue: The Untold Story of Schindler's List*. Other Press, New York, 2005. Translated by David Dollenmayer, 2008.

Revell, Anna. *Oskar Schindler: The True Story of Schindler's List*. Anna Revell, 2017.

Wiesel, Elie. *Night*. Hill and Wang, New York, 1958. Translated by Marion Wiesel, 2006.

<u>Oral History Interviews, Speeches, and Lectures</u>

Jurado, Mary. *Mary Jurado*, oral history conducted January 5, 2021, by Nate Meyers, Chandler Museum.

Meyers, N. (2020, February 29). *Death and Diamonds: The story of Samuel Soldinger* [Lecture]. Chandler Museum Our Stories, Chandler, AZ, USA.

Schindler, O. (1945, May). *The Speech delivered by Schindler to his Jewish workers in Brunnlitz, May 1945, upon the proclamation of the German surrender* [transcript]. Yad Vashem. https://www.yadvashem.org/righteous/stories/schindler/schindler-speech.html

Soldinger, S. (1995, April 25). Recollections of a Schindler Jew [Lecture]. Oregon State University Holocaust Memorial Committee Holocaust Memorial Week 50th Anniversary of Liberation, Milam Auditorium, Corvallis, OR, USA.

Soldinger, Samuel. *Samuel Soldinger – Phoenix Collection*, summary of an oral history conducted May 16, 1989, by an unidentified interviewer, United States Holocaust Memorial Museum, 11 pp.

Soldinger, Samuel. *Samuel Soldinger*, oral history conducted November 12, 1995, by Louise Bobrow, USC Shoah Foundation.

Photographs, Archives, and Objects

Unknown. View of the Alte Schul [Old Synagogue], built in 1407 in the Kazimierz quarter of Krakow. Before 1939, United States Holocaust Memorial Museum/Archiwum Panstwowe w Krakowie, Washington, D.C.

Unknown. A German official supervises a deportation action in the Krakow Ghetto. Jews, assembled in a courtyard with their bundles, await further instructions. C. 1942, United States Holocaust Memorial Museum/Archiwum Panstwowe w Krakowie, Washington, D.C.

Unknown. Forced laborers constructing the wall around the Krakow Ghetto. 1941, United States Holocaust Memorial Museum/Instytut Pamieci Narodowej, Washington, D.C.

Unknown. A column of Jews march with bundles down a main street in Krakow during the liquidation of the ghetto. SS guards oversee the deportation. March 1943, United States Holocaust Memorial Museum/Instytut Pamieci Narodowej, Washington, D.C.

Unknown. A section of the Plaszow concentration camp. 1943-1944, United States Holocaust Memorial Museum/Leopold Page Photographic Collection, Washington, D.C.

Unknown. A member of the German SS supervises the boarding of Jews onto trains during a deportation action in the Krakow Ghetto. C. 1941-1942, United States Holocaust Memorial Museum/Archiwum Dokumentacji Mechanicznej, Washington, D.C.

Titsch, Raimund. Commandant Amon Goeth rides his horse in the Plaszow concentration camp. March 1943 – September 1944, United States Holocaust Memorial Museum/Leopold Page Photographic Collection, Washington, D.C.

Unknown. The entrance to Oskar Schindler's Emalia enamelworks at 4 Lipowa Street in Krakow-Zablocie. 1943-1944, United States Holocaust Memorial Museum/Leopold Page Photographic Collection, Washington, D.C.

Unknown. Oskar Schindler with his horse on the grounds of the Emalia enamelworks in Krakow-Zablocie. United States Holocaust Memorial Museum/Leopold Page Photographic Collection, Washington, D.C.

Unknown. Oskar Schindler at a dinner party in Krakow. At parties
like this, Schindler made contact with various SS and German officials,
which often led to tips about impending deportations that enabled him
to save his laborers. April 28, 1942, United States Holocaust Memorial
Museum/Leopold Page Photographic Collection, Washington, D.C.

Unknown. Prisoners carry large stones up the "stairs of death"
(Todesstiege) from the Wiever Graben quarry at the Mauthausen
concentration camp. 1942, United States Holocaust Memorial
Museum/Archive der KZ-Gedenkstaette Mauthausen, Washington,
D.C.

Albert Abramson. An American tank rolls down the main street of the
Mauthausen concentration camp. May 5, 1945. United States Holocaust
Memorial Museum, courtesy of Albert Abramson, Washington, D.C.

Unknown. A diamond cutter at work at the Chandler Harry Winston
diamond plant. C. 1970. Chandler Museum/Samuel Soldinger
Collection, Chandler, AZ.

Unknown. A room full of diamond cutters at work in the Chandler
Harry Winston plant. C. 1970. Chandler Museum/Samuel Soldinger
Collection, Chandler, AZ.

Unknown. Harry Winston plant in Chandler. C. 1963, Chandler
Museum/Samuel Soldinger Collection, Chandler, AZ.

Unknown. Portrait of Harry Winston. Unknown date, Chandler
Museum/Samuel Soldinger Collection, Chandler, AZ.

Unknown. Samuel Soldinger seated at his desk. C. 1965, Chandler
Museum/Samuel Soldinger Collection, Chandler, AZ.

Unknown. Samuel Soldinger seated at his desk. Unknown date,
Chandler Museum/Samuel Soldinger Collection, Chandler, AZ

Unknown. Samuel Soldinger stands in front of the Harry Winston
plant in Chandler. Unknown date, Chandler Museum/Samuel
Soldinger Collection, Chandler, AZ.